Developing
a Quality
Curriculum

Developing a Quality Curriculum

Allan A. Glatthorn

WAVELAND
PRESS, INC.
Long Grove, Illinois

For information about this book, contact:
   Waveland Press, Inc.
   4180 IL Route 83, Suite 101
   Long Grove, IL 60047-9580
   (847) 634-0081
   info@waveland.com
   www.waveland.com

10-digit ISBN 1-57766-340-3
13-digit ISBN 978-1-57766-340-9

Printed in the United States of America

9   8   7   6   5   4   3

Developing a Quality Curriculum

Foreword

We encounter discussions of "quality" in many contexts today, from television news stories that lament declining standards in business and society to graduate-school textbooks on the philosophy of W. Edwards Deming and the Total Quality Management (TQM) movement. Education has not been immune from these debates, and no doubt you, like your ASCD colleagues, have confronted questions of quality ranging from the caliber of this year's graduating class to whether or not TQM can—or should—be adapted to school management.

Perhaps our reflections about quality can become clearer when we step away from perennial arguments and specific theories to simply consider a basic definition of the word: excellence. This is surely a goal we'd like to achieve for all students and in all areas of education, and it's certainly one of the primary goals that Allan Glatthorn applies to the vital underpinning of all we do in education: the curriculum.

The book you hold in your hands is more than research, more than another theoretical discussion about curriculum. In *Developing a Quality Curriculum*, Glatthorn has blended both research and theory with his many years of hands-on work in the schools to create a quality-oriented approach to curriculum. He does not advocate a single theory of quality; he does not impose rigid formulas or structures for achieving curriculum excellence. He does, however, concisely and candidly detail the various committees, processes, and documents that have brought success to many districts—all of which can be adapted to your local needs.

Glatthorn's bottom line for all of this work is more than a quality curriculum process. After all, what use is the best curriculum guide in the world if it's not achieving something positive for students? Glatthorn steadfastly looks to improved student achievement as the critical outcome of the whole curriculum process. Whether you call that excellence, or quality, or just good education, it's what we strive for every day, the mission that keeps us coming to ASCD books like *Developing a Quality Curriculum* to enrich and enhance our professional lives.

ARTHUR W. STELLER
ASCD President, 1994–95

Preface

This book is written for educational leaders at all levels—state, district, school, and classroom—who want to understand and effectively practice the curriculum development process. It is not a book of curriculum theory or criticism, although such works have an important place in the literature. It is, frankly, a "how-to-do-it" book explaining processes that I believe represent a synthesis of sound research and my own years of experience in consulting with a variety of school systems and schools.

Several basic beliefs that inform this work should be noted here. First, I believe that the state has a legitimate right to identify educational goals and to provide frameworks to accomplish those goals. Second, I believe that the district has an educational need to develop curriculum materials that ensure equity and coordination across the district.

Next, I support the concept of school-based management and believe that schools should use the district guides in developing their own versions of and approaches to the districtwide curriculum. I also firmly believe that classroom teachers should have significant input into the development of district and school curriculum materials and should have a large measure of autonomy in determining how curriculum should be integrated and delivered. Finally, I believe that the excellent curriculum materials developed nationally by federally funded projects should be appropriately used and incorporated into the district's curriculum.

Obviously these assumptions and beliefs run counter to the ideas promulgated by those who believe that each school should develop its own curriculum materials without regard for district requirements or who hold that curriculum making is the sole province of the classroom teacher. Both the research I know and the experience I have gained convince me that a comprehensive, multilevel, and multisource process is most effective.

Most of what I have learned about curriculum work has come from my continued involvement with school districts and educational leaders interested in improving their curriculums. I therefore acknowledge my indebtedness to all of those organizations and individuals. I am especially grateful to the participants in the Massachusetts Commonwealth

Leadership Academy. These colleagues and friends were especially helpful in challenging me, giving me constructive input, and providing useful feedback.

I also wish to acknowledge several colleagues who closely reviewed and gave constructive feedback on a first draft of this work. Especially helpful were Jerry Everhart, science educator, East Carolina University; Lynn Bradshaw, director of human resource development of the Nash County/Rocky Mount (N.C.) School District. Dr. Bradshaw made a significant contribution to the work by carefully critiquing a first draft and suggesting several major and useful changes. I also wish to acknowledge my indebtedness to Ron Brandt, a longtime friend and respected colleague who first suggested the need for this work.

Finally, I dedicate this book to Barbara Glatthorn—spouse, mentor, and friend.

ALLAN A. GLATTHORN

1

Getting Started

You've picked up this book because you're interested in creating a high-quality curriculum process for your district and schools. While we certainly need books on curriculum theory and criticism, many of us are chiefly concerned with practice—with understanding clearly how to do curriculum work. To that end, this book emphasizes the **practical** aspects of how your school system can improve through high-quality curriculum work.

In addition, this work is **research-based**, and, wherever possible, I draw on the best of current research for guidance. Where I draw upon my experience in consulting with more than one hundred school systems, I make clear that a recommendation reflects my research into my own practice, not the empirical research of other scholars.

The book is also **integrative**: it represents a synthesis of several current initiatives and trends. At every stage of development, the book emphasizes the importance of quality of both process and product, which is the most significant aspect of the current interest in "total quality education." (See Bonstingl 1992 for a fuller discussion of the principles of Total Quality Management—TQM—as applied to educational practice.) The curriculum development model presented in Chapter 4 emphasizes the importance of outcomes that are linked through several levels of curriculum work—a major contribution of Spady's "Outcome-Based Education" (see Spady and Marshall 1991). The explanation of unit development found in Chapter 8 is based on the current constructivist model of learning, strongly supported by recent research in thinking and problem solving (see Brooks and Brooks 1993). That same unit model explains how to develop interdisciplinary curriculums that integrate skills and knowledge from several disciplines. Interest in integrated curriculums seems to be on the increase, as evidenced by the number of publications and training programs from the Association for Supervision and Curriculum Development and other professional groups (for one of the most current of these publications, see Drake 1993).

Finally, the book attempts to be **comprehensive** by showing you in very specific ways how your curriculum work can draw upon the best of several sources: state frameworks, major national curriculum projects, the recommendations of experts, and the recommendations of classroom teachers. In doing so, it recognizes the reality that curriculum making is a nested process. The state sets the boundaries in its frameworks; the district explicates the goals and objectives for all students; the school develops a program of studies based upon district goals; and the classroom teacher implements and adds to the district curriculum, in the process developing courses and units that operationalize the district objectives. Before you delve into these details of curriculum work, it will be helpful to have a big picture of what the book covers.

Understanding the Tasks Ahead

Chapter 2 details the several types of groups and the planning needed to accomplish curriculum work. As Chapter 3 explains, certain foundation documents are also needed: curriculum policies, curriculum goals, and a vision of curriculum excellence. With these foundations in place, the district Task Forces then produce and evaluate the scope-and-sequence charts and the curriculum guides needed for quality teaching; Chapter 4 explains these processes.

District work under the direction of the Curriculum Planning Council continues with three major steps. First, you align the curriculum and develop monitoring procedures (Chapter 5). Second, you take the steps necessary to ensure successful implementation (Chapter 6). Finally, with the district curriculum generally in place, work shifts to the school level (Chapter 7). As explained in Chapter 8, the classroom teacher plays a critical role in developing courses, units of study, and yearly plans. The effectiveness of all this work is assessed through a "bottom-line" audit, described in the final chapter.

Assessing the District's Needs

Which of the above processes does your district need to emphasize? A relatively simple needs assessment can help you answer this question by determining the specific tasks you need to accomplish and their priorities. The needs assessment will also enable you to make more effective use of this book.

First, reflect on each statement listed in Figure 1.1 as it applies to your district, and indicate a need by placing a checkmark in the "Need" column. Then review all the items checked to assess their relative priority. Place one of these numbers in the "Priority" column: 1, high priority; 2, middle priority; 3, low priority. Use the results to plan your next steps and use them to decide which chapters of this book you and your colleagues wish to examine most closely.

Ensuring Total Quality Throughout the Curriculum Process

This book continually emphasizes quality: quality processes and quality products. Because of the importance of the issue, it would be useful to consider the concept of a "total quality curriculum," imbued with the basic principles of Total Quality Management.

TQM embodies the theories and practices of W. Edwards Deming (1986) and has been used effectively in the corporate world. It is now frequently touted as the best way to reform the schools (see, for example, Bonstingl 1992). Not all educators, however, are convinced.

Prawat (1993) is one of many critics who believe that a focus on products is antithetical to the development of learning communities, where process matters more. And Capper and Jamison (1993) question the basic values of TQM. Given the fact that TQM appears to embody many educationally desirable principles, however, it would seem useful to determine how the core principles and processes of TQM could be applied to the curriculum development process.

In making such a determination, the current literature provides little help. Bonstingl's (1992) handbook makes only brief reference to the curriculum, and Glasser's (1992) discussion of the "quality curriculum" recommends only that the curriculum teach useful knowledge and skills and emphasize the application of that knowledge and those skills. Part of the problem, obviously, is that TQM's brief educational history means

FIGURE 1.1
Assessing District Needs

Following are the organizational components needed to accomplish effective curriculum work. Indicate a need by placing a check in the "Need" column. Prioritize the checked items with the following scale: 1, high priority; 2, middle priority; 3, low priority. Use the results to plan next steps or to decide which chapters of this book to examine more closely. (Related chapters are noted in parentheses.)

COMPONENTS	NEED	PRIORITY
1. Does the district have an organizational structure for central curriculum planning? (Chapter 2)		
2. Does the district have an organizational structure for developing curriculums? (Chapter 2)		
3. Does the district have an organizational structure for securing citizen input regarding curriculums? (Chapter 2)		
4. Does the district have a long-term plan for developing curriculums? (Chapter 2)		
5. Does the district require groups developing curriculums to submit specific plans for accomplishing that task, and are those plans monitored? (Chapter 2)		
6. Does the board have written policies delineating its role in curriculum development and providing guidance to district educators? (Chapter 3)		
7. Does the district have written curriculum goals? (Chapter 3)		
8. Does the district have a written vision of excellence for curriculum? (Chapter 3)		
9. Does the district have a systematic process for developing and evaluating curriculums, and is that process explicated in writing? (Chapter 4)		
10. Does the district have a systematic process for aligning instruction with the written curriculum and with texts and tests? (Chapter 5)		
11. Does the district have a systematic process for monitoring the curriculum? (Chapter 5)		
12. Does the district have a systematic process for implementing the curriculum? (Chapter 6)		
13. Does each school have its own goals, vision, and written program of studies? (Chapter 7)		
14. Do classroom teachers develop yearly plans, courses of study, and integrated units? (Chapter 8)		
15. Has the district recently conducted an audit that assesses the quality of the delivered curriculum? (Chapter 9)		

there is no empirical evidence available on the effectiveness of TQM as applied to educational problems. The following discussion, therefore, is a preliminary attempt to synthesize the basic principles and processes of Total Quality Management and the current research on education in a way that will make sense to educational leaders. The objective is to remain true to the spirit of TQM without attempting to make a literal translation of a management system originally designed for the corporate world.

I used a systematic process to accomplish this goal, beginning with a close reading of the basic TQM literature, especially those works concerned with the application of TQM to schools. The following sources were most helpful: Aguayo 1990, Deming 1986, Bonstingl 1992, Glasser 1992, and Smith and Hindi 1992. Next, I reviewed the current research on student achievement, drawing chiefly from Wang, Haertel, and Walberg (1993). Finally, I analyzed current theory and research on curriculum to identify the salient characteristics of curriculum quality. From these analyses, I identified common principles and major attributes as a framework for this discussion. In this context, it should be emphasized that I made no attempt to force a fit between TQM and previously advocated models of school reform, such as "Effective Schools," "Site-Based Management," and "Outcome-Based Education." To do so might seem to imply that TQM is an ever-expanding amorphous structure without its own unique characteristics.

The Foundation Principles

The foundation principles provide a basis for the entire improvement effort and establish general guidelines for achieving total quality.

1. A focus on student learning. The focus is on student learning, broadly defined in terms of complex and comprehensive growth. The learned curriculum is the object of ultimate concern; the teacher's planning, the written guide, the textbooks, and the tests are seen as means, not as ends. Any innovation is judged on the basis of its contribution to learning. Resources (time, money, materials) are allocated and expended in a manner that will optimize student learning.

2. An emphasis on quality. District leaders, school administrators, teachers, students, and parents are vitally concerned with quality (not with quantity) and with depth of learning (not with coverage). The curriculum guide and all its supporting documents are of high professional quality, and quality learning is at the heart of all the school's efforts. Students learn in their classes to develop pride of scholarship; the teacher sets high expectations and provides the support for students to achieve quality.

3. Constancy of purpose and continuous improvement. District leaders, school administrators, and teachers develop and implement long-term plans for continuous improvement, especially in the area of curriculum. They avoid "quick fixes," instead acknowledging that meaningful change will take much time and money. They have developed curriculum processes, schedules, and mechanisms that will ensure continuous improvement of the curriculum.

The Core Processes

The core processes are the essential tools for achieving high-quality learning.

1. Dynamic shared leadership. The district provides dynamic, supportive, and coordinating leadership that ensures a concerted movement toward curricular excellence. District leaders develop the needed policies and plans to accomplish quality curriculum work; the principal plays an active role in mobilizing, energizing, and orchestrating the efforts of teachers and students to bring about meaningful change and the successful implementation of curriculums. Leadership and responsibility are shared, however, so that all affected by decisions have input into the process; teachers have considerable influence on the curriculum development process at all stages.

2. Data-based problem solving and decision making. All those providing leadership make major decisions using a problem-solving approach that draws from systematic data, sound research, and informed practice. Curriculums are grounded in sound research on student development and the nature of learning, and they emphasize data-based problem solving for students.

3. Cooperation and teamwork. Cooperative processes are used by leadership teams, instructional teams, and learning groups in developing and implementing the curriculum. The content of the curriculum guides emphasizes the value of cooperation and teamwork.

4. Systematic professional development. District leaders provide districtwide professional development for school administrators and teachers, especially to assist them in the successful implementation of curriculum. The principal and teachers work together to bring about their individual and collective development. High-quality staff development, delivered in quality time, is provided to support curriculum reform. Peers work together to give one another feedback and acquire the new skills and knowledge required by the new curriculum. Close supervision and evaluation by the principal are provided only to those needing it.

2

Organizing and Planning for Curriculum Work

The first consideration in managing the curriculum is how you and your colleagues will organize and plan your work. This chapter suggests some structures and planning processes used successfully in other school systems that can provide a basis for your own decisions about such matters.

Organizing for Success

The types of committees and task forces a school system needs for effective curriculum work will vary, of course, with the size of the district and the resources available. The following organizational structures, outlined in Figure 2.1, seem to be effective for many educators. These recommendations are drawn from my experiences with numerous school systems, and you will want to review and modify them for local use.

Citizens Curriculum Advisory Council

One way to appropriately involve citizens in the area of curriculum is through a Citizens Curriculum Advisory Council. Such a Council is composed of representatives from key constituencies in the community,

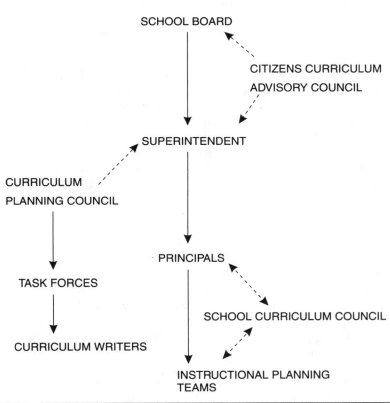

FIGURE 2.1
Relationship of Curriculum Groups

with the superintendent and assistant superintendent for curriculum serving as professional representatives for, and liaisons with, professional educators in the district.

Council members should be appointed by the school board with input from the superintendent and principals. From the start, representatives must understand their responsibilities, particularly the fact that they act in an advisory capacity to the school board. This arrangement preserves the board's legally constituted authority for curriculum. For example, the council could be asked to:

• Advise the board on curriculum policy.
• Foster communication by meeting with individuals and community groups concerned about the curriculum.

• Hold hearings on controversial curriculum issues that affect the community, transmitting recommendations to the board.

• Confer with the Curriculum Planning Council and individual Task Forces to convey community beliefs and opinions about curricular issues.

Observe that the list does not include direct involvement in the curriculum development or evaluation processes. Although some districts prefer to have a more active council that is directly involved in these functions, most educators consider curriculum development and evaluation to be professional functions requiring a great deal of expertise.

If your district already has a broad-based and active citizens advisory council that has more general responsibilities, you could add curriculum advisement to its charge rather than set up a separate group.

Curriculum Planning Council

The Curriculum Planning Council serves as the chief management group for identifying curriculum needs, developing a curriculum calendar, evaluating the curriculum, and appointing and monitoring the work of curriculum task forces. The Planning Council should include representatives of the following constituencies: central office staff, school administrators, professional support staff, and teachers. The superintendent should appoint members with input from central office staff and school principals. In general, members should be selected for their knowledge of the district, their ability to plan, their knowledge of current curriculum practices, and their credibility with colleagues.

Specific tasks for the Curriculum Planning Council are listed below in the order in which they would ordinarily be done. Some tasks may be optional, depending on local preferences. And while these tasks are the formal responsibility of the Planning Council, Council members should always secure input from central office staff, school administrators, and classroom teachers.

1. Organize the Planning Council, setting a schedule, choosing leadership, and determining how decisions will be made.

2. Provide leadership in identifying educational goals and developing a vision of a curriculum of excellence.

3. Explicate the process that the district will use in developing each curriculum guide.

4. Develop and submit budget recommendations for curriculum work.

5. Arrange for needed leadership training and staff development.

6. Identify a standard format for the curriculum guides.

7. Identify and implement curriculum evaluation processes.

8. Develop processes and materials to ensure that the curriculum is effectively implemented.

9. Conduct a needs assessment to identify priorities for developing curriculum guides and related materials.

10. Appoint and provide training for Task Forces that will develop curriculum guides.

11. Monitor the work of Task Forces.

In many ways, the Curriculum Planning Council is the most significant structure for planning and accomplishing needed curriculum work. The Council should be staffed by high-energy professionals who have a vision of where the school system should be headed. Note that some districts have reorganized their central office supervisors as curriculum designers and planners, thus establishing a permanent Curriculum Planning Council.

Curriculum Task Forces

Most of the actual work of curriculum development will be accomplished by a variety of Curriculum Task Forces. These are professional groups appointed by the Curriculum Planning Council to complete specific projects, such as developing a new K–12 mathematics curriculum. Members are nominated by principals and central office staff, selected by the Planning Council, and officially appointed by the superintendent. They should be chosen on the basis of several criteria:

- Knowledge of the subject area for which they are responsible,
- Ability to produce work on schedule,
- Knowledge of the district's curriculum development processes, and
- Influence with classroom teachers.

Ordinarily, each Task Force will include one principal from each level of schooling, one central office supervisor in the area of development, and several teachers who can work together and produce high-quality work. Chapter 4 details the specific work of these Task Forces.

Curriculum Writers

If a Task Force needs additional help with curriculum development, it may wish to appoint Curriculum Writers with the specific responsibility of writing whatever district materials are needed. In most districts, the Task Force members assume this responsibility. If Curriculum Writers are used, they should be selected for their knowledge of the subject and their ability to write clearly and effectively.

School Curriculum Council

The Curriculum Council is the school-based group, composed of school administrators and teacher-leaders, that makes the major decisions concerning school-based curriculum development. Its members provide leadership in program restructuring and development tasks and also develop guidelines for Instructional Planning Teams. If the school already has a leadership team in place, you may have no need for a separate Curriculum Council. (See Chapter 7 for a fuller explanation of the Council's work.)

Instructional Planning Teams

These are teachers in a particular school who work together as a team, cooperating on the tasks they believe necessary for implementing the curriculum effectively. The work of the Instructional Planning Teams is further explained in Chapter 8, but in general they should:
- Develop yearly plans based on the curriculum guide.
- Develop units of study derived from the guide and the yearly plan.
- Develop materials to individualize the curriculum.
- Develop and share learning materials to be used in the classroom.

Planning for Curriculum Work

Each district should have both a general long-term plan for curriculum work and more detailed plans for each curriculum project. The long-term plan typically is developed by the Curriculum Planning Council and reviewed by district and school leaders; the detailed project plans are developed by the appropriate Task Forces and reviewed by the Council.

Developing a General Long-Term Plan

The specific processes a district uses to develop its long-term plan for curriculum work will obviously be affected by such matters as the available resources, the actions of state education departments, the preferences of the local school board, and the district's needs. The following method for developing a long-term plan has worked effectively in many districts and can be the basis for your locally developed planning process.

Begin by determining the length of the planning cycle. Some districts use a five-year cycle, congruent with state adoption of textbooks. Given the rapid pace of change and the frequent turnover of leadership, you might want to use a three-year cycle that is reviewed every year and modified on the basis of current data.

Next, determine which components of the curriculum will be included. A good plan includes periodic development of curriculum materials for all the subjects offered by the school district. The plan may also schedule renewal projects that fine-tune existing guides and offer systematic review of the schools' programs of study.

Third, determine a basic method for setting curriculum planning targets. The choices available are:

• The district sets a regular cycle based on such predetermined factors as textbook adoption sequences, accreditation reviews, and state mandates.

• The district develops a comprehensive strategic plan, with the results used to set curriculum planning priorities.

• The district conducts a comprehensive needs assessment and sets priorities based upon that assessment.

• District and school leaders make their own informal assessments, factoring in such data as national trends and developments, obvious obsolescence or lack of curriculum guides, textbook adoption cycles, and standardized and state test scores.

• The district conducts a curriculum audit and uses the results to develop a long-term plan.

One of these methods will help you set your curriculum planning targets. In setting those targets, you may wish to use the following four stages to emphasize certain tasks year by year:

Planning embraces all the preliminary steps necessary to produce a high-quality curriculum document: appointing Task Forces, developing the knowledge base, orienting teachers, developing Hallmarks of Excellence (this process is explained in Chapter 4), and collecting data and input from teachers.

Production encompasses the actual manufacture of all materials: making scope-and-sequence charts; developing curriculum guides; and creating any other materials required to enable or support the guides.

Piloting includes all activities necessary to use the new materials on a test basis to collect evaluation data and make necessary modifications. When time is not available for comprehensive piloting, individual teachers may be asked to test selected units.

Implementation describes the time when the new curriculum will be put into place and used.

All of the preceding decisions should be transferred to a long-term planning chart. One useful form lists all the programs of study and all the courses on the left-hand side. The school years covered by the plan are listed across the top. In the columns below, the appropriate stage is noted, as demonstrated in Figure 2.2.

Our model

FIGURE 2.2
Sample Long-Term Planning Chart

	SCHOOL YEARS			
SUBJECTS	**1994–95**	**1995–96**	**1996–97**	**1997–98**
Art	Plan	Produce	Pilot	Implement
English Language Arts		Plan	Produce	Pilot
Foreign Language			Plan	Produce
Home Economics	Plan Produce	Pilot	Implement	
Social Studies				Plan

Once this chart is completed, the Curriculum Planning Council should review the tentative decisions, considering the following issues:

- Does the plan reflect the district's priority needs?
- Has enough time been provided for each project?
- Are needed resources available?
- Does the plan reflect an appropriate pace of change, given the district resources and needs?
- Does the plan avoid overloading elementary teachers with several new guides in a single year?

That last issue is most crucial. Elementary teachers usually teach five or six different subjects; as a result, they feel overwhelmed when an overly ambitious curriculum plan requires them to implement one or two new guides each year (see Marsh and Odden 1991 for details about this problem). Also keep in mind that, in general, it is wiser to complete a smaller number of high-quality projects than a larger number of mediocre ones.

After the plan is revised by the Curriculum Planning Council, it should be reviewed by all who will be directly affected. Their input should be used to prepare a final draft for board adoption.

Creating a Specific Project Plan

Once the long-term plan is developed, the Task Force responsible for a specific curriculum project should create a detailed plan for accomplishing its work. One useful process is described here, using as an example a Task Force appointed to develop a new K–12 mathematics guide:

1. Determine if the project plan will focus on one of the stages of development (planning, production, piloting, implementation) or on two or more. Also determine what time period the plan will cover. In this example, the mathematics Task Force has decided to develop a one-year plan covering both planning and production.

2. Identify the components to be included in the plan. Following are the elements that seem to be needed in the planning and production stages, along with the specific steps that are usually involved:

– *Administration.* Submitting proposals, making reports, securing resources, holding meetings, noting target dates.

– *Knowledge development.* Reviewing and synthesizing the research, noting exemplary projects, synthesizing expert recommendations.

– *Data Collection.* Compiling input from classroom teachers on what should be emphasized for mastery grade by grade.

– *Staff Development.* Orienting faculty to the project, training principals and supervisors, training users of the guide.

– *Materials Production.* Developing data collection forms, developing a scope-and-sequence chart, writing grade-level objectives, developing curriculum-based tests, and producing other needed materials.

– *Materials Selection.* Choosing the texts, software, and multimedia required for the new guide.

– *Evaluation.* Evaluating the staff development, the materials produced, and other program components.

3. Make a modified Gantt chart. In the left column, list the major elements of the planning processes needed for that stage of curriculum work. Across the top row, list the months that will be covered by the plan, and in the columns below, detail specific tasks, as demonstrated in Figure 2.3.

FIGURE 2.3
Sample Project Planning Chart

	AUG.	SEPT.	OCT.	NOV.	DEC.
ADMINISTRATION	Submit plan to CPC	Principals review plan	Hold first meeting		
KNOWLEDGE DEVELOPMENT			Begin research synthesis		

4. Complete the planning chart by thinking about the target dates for the project, available resources, possible constraints, and the pace of development that seems most appropriate. In making these decisions, keep in mind that the summer months are the best time for intensive materials production and for many components of staff development.

5. Have the planning chart reviewed by all those who will be affected and make appropriate modifications.

As you organize this work, remember that your aim is to facilitate improvement, not to create another level of inflexible bureaucracy. Keep the structures simple and the plans flexible, and you'll be on your way to comprehensive, well-organized curriculum change.

3

Laying the Foundations for the District Curriculum

Early in the process of developing curriculums, the Curriculum Planning Council should provide leadership in developing three foundation statements and making one major decision that will guide future work. The first foundation statement is the district's curriculum policy; the second, a formulation of the district's educational goals; the third, a statement of vision of a curriculum of excellence. Obviously the three are closely related, and they will complement a major decision regarding the focus and emphasis of curriculum guides: Will the district focus on a mastery curriculum?

Consider this analogy. The educational goals are the learning destinations you hope the students will reach. The vision is your dream of the high-powered vehicle that will best take them there. And the policy is the body of laws governing how you will accomplish the journey.

Which of these tasks you accomplish first will depend on several factors: the availability of existing materials (such as state goals), the preferences of the Council members, and the press of other responsibilities. Developing the policies first and then the goal statement is the choice recommended here. Development of the vision and a decision about the mastery focus can both come later.

Developing a Curriculum Policy

As Elmore and Sykes (1992, p. 186) define the term, curriculum policy is "the formal body of law and regulation that pertains to what should be taught in schools." Research indicates that such policies generally have little effect on student achievement (see Wang, Haertel, and Walberg 1993). Despite this limitation, it seems desirable for the school board to provide a legal basis for its control by adopting a general policy affirming its authority over curriculum.

English (1992) recommends a comprehensive set of board policies covering such matters as curriculum alignment, testing, textbook adoption, budget development, curriculum roles and responsibilities, equity, and public reporting. In his audit process, he expects to find policies addressing twenty-one specific areas, and districts are faulted if they address fewer than fourteen of the total. A simpler process is recommended here. The board should adopt one general curriculum policy, which might read like this:

> 1. The board has responsibility and authority for the school district's curriculum, within the limits specified by the state.
> 2. In discharging this responsibility, it will also approve and adopt all the basic instructional materials required by that curriculum.
> 3. The board assigns to the superintendent of schools the responsibility of developing and implementing the administrative regulations needed to operationalize this policy.

The superintendent and the Curriculum Planning Council can then work together to develop for the board's review the necessary administrative regulations, which would typically include the following:

- The process by which new curriculums will be developed and formally adopted;
- The roles of central office staff, school administrators, and teachers in developing and implementing the curriculum;
- The process for aligning the written curriculum guides with tests and instructional materials;
- The process for monitoring curriculum implementation;
- The means by which curriculum needs are addressed in the budget process;
- The processes by which curriculums will be evaluated;
- The need for ensuring equal access to a high-quality curriculum; and
- The methods by which that equal access will be ensured.

Developing a Statement of Educational Goals

The next foundation document is the statement of educational goals. Educational goals are very general statements of the outcomes you hope students will achieve after completing formal schooling. They are the same as "exit outcomes," the term used in outcome-based education. Here is an example, simply to show the level of generality:

> Communicate clearly and effectively in speaking, writing, and using visual media for a variety of audiences and purposes.

Some districts prefer to use a format that states the general goal first and then identifies several subgoals that compose the general one. For example, Brookover (1980, pp. 9–10) states the "self-concept" goal in this manner:

> *Goal Two: Self-Conceptualization*
> *Subgoals*
> 1. Recognizes that self-concept is required in interaction with other people.
> 2. Distinguishes between significant and nonsignificant others and their self-evaluations.
> 3. Takes into account significant others and disregards nonsignificant others in the self-conceptualizing process.
> 4. Distinguishes among many concepts of self in various roles or social situations.
> 5. Assesses own functioning in each of several different situations.
> 6. Perceives accurately, assesses validly, and responds appropriately to others' evaluations in the context of each specific role situation rather than generalizing to all situations.

Such goals have several uses. They remind educators of what is really essential. They provide a basis for developing and evaluating a school's program of study, as explained in Chapter 7. They give direction in developing the district's curriculum guides. And they provide an excellent basis for developing new performance measures.

Several sources of goals are available. Most states have developed such lists and often require that the goals be explicitly related to all curriculum work. John Goodlad's (1984) work includes an excellent synthesis of the goal statements from several states. Figure 3.1 on page 20 shows a sample set of goals developed explicitly for a middle school; they could easily be modified to serve an entire district.

FIGURE 3.1
Sample Goals for Middle School Learners

Learning Skills
1. Read with understanding and critical judgment.
2. Write clearly and effectively, and use writing as a way to learn.
3. Speak and listen well, especially in structured situations.
4. Use mathematical problem-solving processes.
5. Reason logically and think critically.
6. Study and learn effectively.
7. Use the computer to solve problems, compose, process information.

Basic Academic Subjects
Learn important concepts and the special skills of. . .

8. English language and literature.
9. Mathematics.
10. Science.
11. Foreign language.
12. Social studies.
13. The arts.

Health and Physical Education
14. Understand the nature and importance of physical and mental health.
15. Develop physical fitness and recreation skills.

Creative Thinking and Expression
16. Express ideas and images creatively in a variety of media.
17. Think creatively and solve problems creatively.

Personal Skills and Attitudes
18. Develop positive self-image.
19. Make sound moral decisions.
20. Develop special interests and leisure activities.
21. Cope with changes in family, community, society.
22. Make sound decisions about careers, finances, use of media, and other important personal issues.
23. Develop desirable attitudes toward work and study.
24. Develop motivation to learn.

Interpersonal Skills and Attitudes
25. Work cooperatively with others.
26. Value own ethnic identity and respect that of others.
27. Treat others with respect, regardless of age, gender, class, ethnic origin.
28. Become a contributing member of the family.
29. Develop attitudes of responsible citizenship.
30. Develop an awareness of global interdependence.

Source: From *Middle School/Junior High Principal's Handbook* by Allan A. Glatthorn and Norman Spencer, copyright © 1986. Used by permission of the publisher, Prentice Hall/A Division of Simon and Schuster, Englewood Cliffs, N.J.

If your district is in a state that does not mandate the use of state goals, you should develop your own goal list. The superintendent should begin the task by briefing the school board members on the goal-development process and determining how and when they will be involved, since the statement of broad educational goals is clearly one of their responsibilities. The process recommended here is for the professional staff to do the groundwork, presenting the results to the board for their review, modification, and adoption.

The Curriculum Planning Council should provide the leadership in organizing and guiding the project. In doing so, they have several choices as to how to proceed. Some districts begin by holding a series of community meetings, asking participants to identify goals. This approach is recommended by Brandt and Tyler (1983). Meeting participants are reminded of Tyler's (1949) recommendation that educational goals be derived from an analysis of the subject, the society, and the students. They discuss these issues in small groups, identify priority goals, listen to group presentations, and collaborate in synthesizing the small-group work. The same processes are then used by the professional staff members, who produce their own list. The community and the professional lists are then synthesized into one final product.

Other districts have compiled lists of goals from several sources, including curriculum materials from other school systems. This process is efficient, but it leaves the professional staff feeling no sense of ownership. The following process is efficient and also results in locally produced goal statements.

The Curriculum Planning Council begins by analyzing the subjects required in the existing curriculum. Those subjects are required because they implicitly embody your district's goals. For example, mathematics is required because you believe all students should be able to use mathematical concepts and skills in understanding, representing, and solving problems where mathematical reasoning is required.

As the Planning Council considers each required subject in turn, members ask, "What educational goals are assumed to be important by requiring this subject?" Subject-matter specialists can assist in this task. Professional organizations, such as the National Council for the Teaching of Mathematics, are also useful sources for goal statements in a particular subject. As indicated in Figure 3.1, you may wish to group the major subject-related goals together.

With the subject-derived goals identified, the Council should now turn its attention to those goals that have been missed through the subject-analysis process. Essentially they attempt to answer this question: "What else do we want for our students?" This question poses a difficult choice about the breadth and inclusiveness of the goal statement.

Goodlad (1984) points out that citizens have always supported a wide range of goals, and a recent report in the *ERS Spectrum* (Educational Research Service 1992) notes that a survey of more than three thousand principals and a like number of teachers indicated broad support for the "Seven Cardinal Principles" of 1918, which included such goals as "worthy home membership," "worthy use of leisure," and "ethical character." Recent community controversies, however, indicate that many people want the schools to focus on a narrow set of academic goals. The Citizens Curriculum Advisory Council can play a facilitating role here, advising the planners on what they believe the community will support.

The Planning Council should review several sources to help identify goals that do not relate to a particular subject. Goodlad (1984) would be a useful source as would Spady's work on "transformational outcomes" (Spady and Marshall 1991). Also, the goals listed in Figure 3.1 that are not related to a particular subject might be helpful; they represent several educational goals that may have been missed in the subject-analysis process.

Now the Council should determine if any of the goals can be better combined. For example, it is likely that several of the goals refer to critical thinking and creative thinking in the social studies, in mathematics, in science, and so on. Those separate statements could be better combined in one statement similar to the following:

> Think critically and creatively, using theories, models, and concepts from several fields of study.

The results of this work should be organized into a first draft, which should then be submitted to administrators, teachers, and the Citizens Curriculum Advisory Council for review. Minor suggestions should be synthesized into a second draft; major differences will need to be resolved through discussion. This draft should then be submitted to the board for its review.

Once the educational goals have been identified, educators may decide to identify the standards of performance expected at school exit points (grades 5 and 8 for most districts). For example, here is the standard of performance for the communication goal for grade 8:

> In achieving this goal, students will be expected to write the following types of messages, with words spelled correctly and sentences

punctuated correctly: a letter to the editor of the local paper; a personal narrative; a set of directions for someone visiting the local community.

Developing a Vision of Curriculum Excellence

The next step in the process of laying the foundation for quality curriculum work is articulating a vision of a curriculum of excellence for the 21st century. Accomplishing that goal will afford several advantages to you and your colleagues. You will have an opportunity to share your dreams of a curriculum of the future. You will produce a document that can provide visionary guidelines for curriculum work. And the vision will serve to unify disparate efforts around a common dream.

In the process recommended here, the articulation of the vision takes place before the development of curriculums. Note, however, Fullan's (1993) insightful conclusion that the best visions often emerge from practice. This suggests that you and your colleagues should develop a preliminary and tentative statement of your curriculum vision, one that will guide early work. Then revise that vision as you gain more experience.

Some districts prefer to develop a philosophy statement instead of a vision. The statement of philosophy comprises the general beliefs held by educators, especially as they affect curriculum. A vision statement seems more useful than a philosophy statement because it looks ahead and sets targets for development teams.

The task of developing the vision should be accomplished under the leadership of the members of the Curriculum Planning Council. Who they involve will depend on the size of the district and how much time is to be devoted to the task. Obviously, administrators and teachers should all be involved in the process; parents can play a role; and some school systems have included secondary students.

The process explained here should be adapted to meet the needs of your district. This approach is a modification of the "nominal group process," which asks individuals to work on their own first and then synthesizes individual efforts into a group result. (For a fuller explanation of the nominal group process, see Moore 1987.) The process also represents a "bottom-up" approach in which individual schools develop their own visions of curriculum, which in turn are synthesized into a collective district vision. This process has worked well with medium-sized districts and can be easily adapted to the special nature of your school system.

To begin the process, the Planning Council synthesizes the knowledge base for the vision, preparing a document that highlights these developments:

- The changing nature of society and your community,
- The changing nature of students,
- New developments in technology, and
- Current research on teaching, learning, and curriculum. (Hodgkinson 1992 is an excellent source of information about national trends.)

Each school then uses the knowledge base in developing its vision of curriculum. The principal serves as leader throughout the process, assisted by group facilitators who have received special training. On a district inservice day, each school faculty works with representative parents to develop a vision. They begin by discussing the knowledge base provided by the Planning Council. Following this discussion, participants are divided into small groups of five to seven. Each member of the group is given the following task:

> Working alone, without discussion, think about the knowledge base and your dream of a curriculum. Identify several key adjectives that catch the flavor of the kind of curriculum you want. Here are some examples: meaningful, challenging, equitable. . . . Write at least seven and no more than ten such adjectives. Focus on those that reflect the key attributes of the curriculum you desire.

When the participants have finished that task, they are then given these directions:

> Now go back and refine your brainstormed list. Cross out any that give you second thoughts. Combine any that can be combined. Find alternative phrasings when that seems desirable. Reduce your list to the five most important adjectives.

When that task has been completed, the facilitator of each group collects each participant's adjectives in a round-robin manner, listing them on newsprint. The group then discusses each, clarifying terms and analyzing their importance. Following the discussion, each member casts 15 votes, distributing them among the adjectives that seem most important to the vision.

The facilitator tallies the results of the balloting and notes the ten adjectives that have received the highest totals. Each group takes each adjective in turn and develops it into a sentence that states clearly that element of the vision. For example:

MULTICULTURAL. The curriculum reflects and responds to the cultural diversity of this nation and our community, so that students develop a sense of pride in their own heritage and a respect for that of others.

GOAL-BASED. The curriculum focuses on significant goals, so that students develop the critical skills and acquire the knowledge they need for effective lifelong learning and full functioning as citizens in a changing society.

Each group then reviews its comprehensive statement to ensure that it really reflects their vision of excellence. Now it is time for group reporting. Each group posts its vision of curriculum, and the lists are compared to note common elements and discuss seemingly discrepant components. The meeting adjourns with the principal asking for feedback about the process and explaining the next steps.

During the week that follows, the facilitators of each group meet to review all the reports. They again identify the common elements and synthesize them into the first draft of the school's vision of curriculum. That first draft is shared with the faculty and the parent representatives, who are asked to provide feedback. If the feedback suggests general support, the principal incorporates suggestions for minor revisions into a final statement. If the feedback indicates major disagreement, those issues are discussed and resolved in a follow-up meeting.

Each school then submits its vision of the curriculum to the Planning Council. They identify common elements, discuss discrepancies, and prepare a draft of the district's vision, which is then sent back to the schools for review, discussion, and feedback. The Council uses the feedback to develop a revised draft, which is then submitted to the board. A sample of one such document is shown as Figure 3.2 on page 26—not as a model but as an example of what such a vision can look like.

The final district vision statement will be used as a touchstone for all future curriculum work, though each school retains its own vision as a guide to any special curriculum projects undertaken by that faculty. (See Chapter 7 for further details.)

Some feel that the process of developing a vision is an unnecessary waste of time, producing meaningless rhetoric that has little value. My experience suggests otherwise. Districts that have taken the process seriously report that the discussions were meaningful exchanges and that the final product was used as a checklist for guiding curriculum development.

FIGURE 3.2
Sample Vision Statement

The Washington City Schools' Vision of Curriculum

We, the educators of the Washington City School System, hold forth this vision of the curriculum of excellence we desire for all our students. We have a dream of a curriculum that is . . .

1. MEANINGFUL. The curriculum emphasizes the active construction of meaning, so that all students find purpose in their studies.

2. TECHNOLOGICAL. The curriculum uses technology as one delivery system, examines the influence of technology on students' lives, and gives students the skills they need to use the technology to accomplish their own purposes.

3. SOCIALLY RESPONSIBLE. The curriculum develops in students a sense of social responsibility, so that they become aware of their obligations and duties as citizens in a democracy and are especially sensitive to the needs of the poor and the aged.

4. MULTICULTURAL. The curriculum reflects and is responsive to the cultural diversity of this nation and our community, so that students develop a sense of pride in their own heritage and a respect for that of others.

5. REFLECTIVE. The curriculum fosters in students the skills and attitudes of reflection, so that they are able to think critically, creatively, and affirmatively.

6. HOLISTIC. The curriculum gives appropriate emphasis to all the significant aspects of growth and all the types of human intelligence, helping students see the connections between the separate subjects.

7. GLOBAL. The curriculum develops in students an awareness of global interdependence in all aspects of life, including the environment and the economy.

8. OPEN-ENDED. The curriculum is open-ended in two ways: it is open to revision and continued refinement; and it provides open access to all students, so that students are not tracked into dead-end careers.

9. GOAL-BASED. The curriculum focuses on significant goals, so that students develop the critical skills and acquire the knowledge they need for effective lifelong learning and full functioning as citizens in a changing society.

Choosing a Curriculum Focus

Will all district guides focus on the mastery curriculum, or will they have a more comprehensive perspective? This is the major decision that must be made at the outset of your curriculum work. A mastery curriculum focuses on essential learnings that will require explicit planning, teaching, and testing; such a curriculum deliberately avoids explicit attention to enrichment content or to affective outcomes that should be nurtured on every appropriate occasion.

To understand the concept of the mastery curriculum, you need to analyze all curriculums in terms of two constructs: importance and structure. Some knowledge and skills seem to have high importance for all students, and they are the essential learnings that all students need to master. These include the major concepts, principles, ideas, and skills of any subject. But knowledge and skills with less importance are of the "trivial pursuit" variety: specific facts about minor elements and skills that are not considered essential.

For example, knowing the causes of the Civil War would seem to be important for all students. Knowing the details of one of the minor skirmishes would seem to have low importance. Knowing how to write an effective business letter is a skill of high importance; knowing how to diagram a sentence is one of low importance.

Learning can also be analyzed in terms of its structure. Some learning seems to be of high structure, that is, it is best mastered when the following structural attributes are present:

- It is manifested in specific objectives.
- It is clearly articulated.
- It is well coordinated and sequenced.
- It is carefully assessed.
- It is explicitly taught.

For example, understanding the principles of genetics is learning of high structure; it must be explicitly planned, taught, and tested. But developing scientific curiosity seems to be learning of low structure; it should be nurtured on every suitable occasion, not taught in 5th grade and then forgotten. In the case of developing scientific curiosity, the learning objectives can be more general, coordination and articulation are not crucial, sequence is unimportant, assessment is not necessary or practical, and no explicit teaching seems required.

These two analyses yield four kinds of curriculums, as shown in Figure 3.3: mastery, organic, team-determined enrichment, and student-determined enrichment.

The **mastery curriculum** meets two criteria: it has high importance for all students and high structure in the teaching/learning process. (Some school districts where I have consulted prefer to call this the "core curriculum," since mastery is so closely associated with the "mastery learning" theory of Benjamin Bloom.) This curriculum requires high-quality curriculum guides, standardization across the district, scope-and-sequence charts, and excellent assessment. Note also that the mastery curriculum requires careful planning and explicit teaching. Students will not "pick up on their own" the elements of the mastery curriculum.

The **organic curriculum** has two attributes as well: high importance and low structure. Like the mastery curriculum, it has high importance for all students; experienced educators believe all students should acquire organic learnings. These learnings are possible, however, without all the structuring and organizing of the mastery curriculum. It is nurtured, rather than taught. Consider, for example, this outcome found in many curriculum guides: "Listen attentively and courteously." It describes an organic outcome that should be fostered on every appropriate occasion, not taught in 3rd or 4th grade.

FIGURE 3.3
Types of Curriculums

	IMPORTANCE	
	HIGH	**LOW**
S T R U C T U R E **HIGH**	Mastery Curriculum	Team-Determined Enrichment Curriculum
LOW	Organic Curriculum	Student-Determined Enrichment Curriculum

The **team-determined enrichment curriculum** has low importance and high structure. It is not considered essential for all students. It includes knowledge that is "nice to know" but not critical to understanding a discipline. However, this knowledge has a structure similar to the mastery curriculum. Learnings must be carefully planned and explicitly taught. Thus, this curriculum is best developed by teams of teachers who coordinate their efforts to ensure that "dinosaurs" are not taught as enrichment in grades 1, 2, 3, and 4. Another example of team-determined enrichment is knowing the states represented in the Continental Congress. While that may be of interest to some students, it is not essential to understanding the American Revolution.

The final type of curriculum is **student-determined enrichment**, the low-importance, low-structure curriculum. It is the curriculum generated by students as they raise issues unrelated to the mastery or team-determined component. It is also the curriculum that students generate as they independently pursue their own interests. Obviously, student-determined enrichment cannot be planned before the teacher has met the students for a given year.

Implications for Curriculum Planning

Although the concept of a mastery curriculum is used throughout this book, several school districts have decided not to use it. They worry that it somehow shrinks the curriculum too much or slights important organic outcomes. While I do not believe that such concerns provide sufficient justification for returning to an undifferentiated approach, I believe the issue is so critical that it should be examined thoroughly and systematically by all involved. If you decide that the four types of curriculum represent a useful approach for your school system, this analysis has several implications for your work as a curriculum leader.

First, you acknowledge a need for a high-quality mastery curriculum developed by the school district. While several in the curriculum field believe the move toward school-based management should include school-based curriculum development, such development should be based on a high-quality mastery curriculum that is the same for all schools at a particular level. School-based curriculums developed independent of the district mastery curriculum result in a lack of articulation from level to level and can bring about marked inequities across the system.

Second, keep in mind that district guides should focus solely on the mastery curriculum, leaving ample time for the other three components.

The intent here is to focus teachers' attention on the mastery elements while giving them the latitude they need to nurture organic outcomes and to enrich and remediate. Focusing on the mastery elements also results in a "teacher-friendly" guide that is easy to use.

Also develop implementation strategies that will ensure all students have equal access to the mastery curriculum, for the mastery curriculum is designed to ensure a high-quality curriculum for *all* students. It can serve as the basis for Individualized Educational Plans for special needs students and as the foundation curriculum for gifted and talented students. As Goodlad and Oakes (1988) point out, all students need access to a curriculum that focuses on knowledge that is central, challenging, complex, and rich in meaning.

In developing the mastery curriculum, be sure you do not let it crowd out the other elements. How much time should the mastery curriculum require? The answer depends on both the developmental needs of students and the nature of the subject. In general, most experts recommend that the early grades of schooling involve more of an organic approach, one that gives the teacher a great deal of time to respond to the developing needs of the children, to integrate content as needed, and to nurture positive attitudes towards learning. The later years of formal schooling probably require a more structured mastery approach.

Subjects also seem to differ in this respect. Mathematics, sciences, foreign languages, and vocational-technical subjects seem to require more time for the mastery component. English language arts, social studies, health, physical education, and the arts suggest a more organic approach.

A very rough rule of thumb that I have evolved in working with districts is to develop a mastery curriculum that will require from 60 to 75 percent of classroom time. This approach leaves sufficient time for the organic, enables teams to develop an enrichment curriculum for all students, and provides some limited time for the student-determined. (Note the irony of present practice: schools offer an enrichment curriculum to those who least need it—the gifted—and deny it to those who could best profit from it—the at-risk.) Reducing the scope of the mastery curriculum produces two other benefits. It facilitates in-depth study and problem solving, since there is less content to cover. It also gives the teacher time to provide for individual and group remediation.

Do not ignore the organic curriculum. While it does not require a written guide, it does require systematic attention. You may wish to do what some districts have found useful: develop a set of reminders for all teachers. Figure 3.4 shows one such list developed for English language arts. Be sure you do not rely solely on such lists. Teachers will need staff development that will give them the knowledge and the skills to foster organic outcomes.

FIGURE 3.4
An Organic Curriculum for English Language Arts

As you teach the English language arts, keep in mind the following organic outcomes and nurture them at every appropriate occasion.

Students will come to...

1. Enjoy reading.
2. Value their own dialects and respect the dialects of others.
3. Use language with sensitivity and respect.
4. Value writing as a way of knowing and communicating.
5. Appreciate the dynamic nature of language.
6. Value the contributions of ethnic minorities to our language and literature.
7. Listen attentively and courteously.
8. Speak clearly and courteously in informal communication contexts.

Teachers will also need help in learning how to develop team-determined enrichment units. Such units should be loosely coordinated across grade levels, so that students do not encounter the same enrichment content year after year or find, for example, that the mastery curriculum for 8th grade includes much of what they learned in the 7th grade enrichment units. This loose coordination can be achieved if the teachers of one grade level are helped to develop tentative plans for their enrichment and then scheduled to meet with colleagues in the grade above and below theirs to work out conflicts in a spirit of compromise. The final list of activities should then be checked against the mastery curriculum to ensure that there is no undesirable duplication.

4

Building the Components of the District Curriculum

After you've formulated your foundation statements and decided to pursue a mastery curriculum, you're ready to either *develop* or *renew* the district's K–12 curriculum in a given subject area. *Develop* is used here in the sense of producing a new curriculum guide with supporting materials. *Renew* is used here to identify a process of revising an existing guide. This chapter gives greater attention to the development process, since it is more complex and more frequently used. But you'll find a brief explanation of the renewal process on page 47 at the end of the development discussion.

There is no single best way to develop a new curriculum. The process explained here has worked well with many school systems, but you should also review different approaches. English's 1992 work and Fielding's 1990 monograph seem especially useful. You should also feel free to develop your own approach, since the best process will be sensitive to local needs, talents, and resources. Whatever choice you make, the Curriculum Planning Council should produce a written description of the curriculum development process so all Task Forces follow the same general procedures.

Seeing the Big Picture

Before examining specific processes in detail, you should have a good grasp of the big picture—a map of the field of inquiry. One important piece of that picture is knowing what elements will shape your work. You will be attempting to develop a set of high-quality curriculum materials that will synthesize several elements for a given field of study:

- State frameworks or guidelines
- Exemplary national curriculum projects
- Research on teaching and learning in a subject area
- Research on child and adolescent development
- High-quality commercially produced learning materials
- Your district's educational goals and vision of curriculum
- Supervisor and teacher recommendations

How you integrate these elements will depend on the process you choose. The explanations provided here will help you with this task, but remember that such work is recursive and interactive, not linear, so feel free to use the steps in this chapter flexibly and interactively.

A second piece of the big picture is knowing specifically what you will produce. In the model presented here, you and your colleagues will generate several essential products:

- A list of subject mastery goals, derived from the educational goals and other sources;
- A summary of the knowledge base with a synthesis of research and exemplary practice;
- A statement of "Hallmarks of Excellence" for a given subject, derived from the vision statement and research synthesis;
- The curriculum framework for that subject, identifying the major components of the delivery system;
- The strands of that subject; the recurring components that become part of the scope-and-sequence chart;
- A scope-and-sequence chart, noting the mastery elements for each strand and each grade;
- A list of materials (both professional and commercial) that can be incorporated into the district's curriculum; and
- The curriculum guide.

You may decide to produce other materials, some of which will be explained briefly below. Again, keep in mind that the decision about what to produce should be made by the Curriculum Planning Council as it develops standard procedures for all curriculum work in the district.

The third piece of the big picture is understanding who will carry out the tasks. Identifying subject mastery goals should be done jointly by the Planning Council and subject-matter Task Forces or committees. The rest of the tasks are the responsibility of the subject-matter Task Forces alone. (Review Chapter 2 for a description of the Task Force members and their work.)

The final piece of the big picture is knowing what is not included in the following discussion. First, it is assumed that you will provide staff development throughout this process. While brief mention is made of critical staff development programs, staff development is not treated thoroughly in this book. Second, selection of textbooks is a key decision that is referred to only briefly in the following discussion. Finally, the development of authentic assessments based on the curriculum is absolutely essential, but for reasons of space and focus, it is not treated in this book.

Developing a Mastery Curriculum

The process of developing a mastery curriculum for a given subject is complex. The following discussion explains the steps to take in this process.

1. Identify the Subject Mastery Goals

Subject mastery goals are general statements of the end-states desired—the knowledge and skills in one subject that the mastery curriculum hopes to develop in learners after several years of schooling. These goals should be related to and derived from the general educational goals you previously identified. This connection can be established if the Planning Council takes two important steps to operationalize the educational goals: (1) align goals and programs, and (2) align the mastery curriculum goals and the subjects.

Align Goals and Programs. The first step is to align the goals with the educational programs available. The educational programs are all those experiences provided for all students: the mastery curriculum; the organic curriculum; the hidden curriculum or the culture of the school, as it affects learners; the activity program; and the student services program. This step is especially useful for affective goals, since they might be better achieved through means other than the mastery curriculum.

The process begins with the Planning Council developing a matrix. Down the left side list the educational goals; across the top, record all the educational programs that contribute to them. Through careful deliberation, the Council considers each goal and identifies those programs they think should emphasize this goal, inserting the letter *E* in the appropriate column. Then they decide which other programs should reinforce this goal, using the letter *R* in the matrix. *Emphasize* is used in the sense of "making a significant and focused effort." *Reinforce* is used in the sense of "contributing to and supporting, but not emphasizing."

Here is an example for the goal of "develop a strong sense of self-esteem":

GOAL	MASTERY	ORGANIC	HIDDEN	ACTIVITY	SERVICES
Self-esteem	R	E	E	R	R

These entries indicate that the planners believe the goal of enhancing self-esteem can best be achieved through the organic and hidden curriculums, not the mastery curriculum.

To ensure strong support and involvement, these results should be discussed with the Citizens Curriculum Advisory Council, central office supervisors, all school administrators, and representative groups of teachers. Then make necessary revisions.

This final draft is used in a systematic way. Special committees are charged with developing systematic plans for ensuring that the organic curriculum, the hidden curriculum, the activity program, and the student services program are structured to properly focus on both the "emphasize" and "reinforce" goals.

Align the Mastery Curriculum Goals and the Subjects. After aligning goals and programs, the Planning Council focuses on the mastery curriculum goals, listing those the mastery curriculum will emphasize or reinforce. The list is submitted to all subject Task Forces (or to representative supervisors and teachers where no Task Force exists). The groups are instructed to determine which goals their subject will emphasize and which it will reinforce, again using the symbols *E* and *R*. These are vital decisions, since the choices will be used to identify subject mastery goals and develop curriculum guides.

When the results are collated and presented on a large spreadsheet or chart, they may look something like the following. It's an example of a chart one district developed for the goal of "think critically and analytically" in its mastery curriculum.

GOAL	ART	ENGLISH	HEALTH	HOME EC.	MATH
Critical thinking	R	E	E	R	E

The Planning Council then reviews the results of this process, addressing two issues: Is every mastery curriculum goal appropriately emphasized and reinforced? Does each subject have an appropriate load of goals, attempting neither too little nor too much? Any discrepancies are discussed with the appropriate Task Force.

These two processes have yielded important information for the district: a comprehensive map of how the broad educational goals will be achieved and a clear picture of how the mastery curriculum goals will be achieved, subject by subject. Such results are useful for countering two related problems. First, many leaders err in assuming that all educational goals must be addressed through the mastery curriculum. They therefore rely too much on curriculum and ignore the contributions that other programs can make. Second, too many leaders think that educational goals are empty rhetoric, and they forget about them once they have been identified. This process is a major step in ensuring that such goals are actualized.

2. Analyze State Frameworks

This is a good place for the Task Force to analyze state frameworks and synthesize the information into a clear set of requirements that can guide the district's decision making. As of the time of this writing, forty-five states were planning, developing, or implementing new curriculum frameworks, according to a report issued by the Consortium for Policy Research in Education (1993). Some of those frameworks are very general, specifying only goals and graduation requirements; others are more specific and thus more constraining. Curry and Temple (1992) present this comprehensive list of what state frameworks may include:

- Philosophy, rationale, and goals
- Learner and school outcomes
- Content standards
- Student performance assessment and standards
- Themes and concepts
- Instructional strategies
- Use of technology
- Sample units
- Instructional materials criteria
- Interdisciplinary strategies

3. Refine Subject Mastery Goals

Each subject Task Force now focuses on its list of mastery curriculum goals. To ensure that no major goal has been ignored, members first review the state framework for that subject, exemplary projects, and the recommendations of experts in the field. Principals, supervisors, and teachers in that field then review the Task Force decisions. Any changes emerging from these reviews are submitted to the Planning Council for incorporation into the district's mastery document.

In this way, each Task Force produces its own list of subject mastery goals: those the subject will emphasize and those it will reinforce. This goal document will guide all future work, and it should be evaluated for its quality to ensure that it is clear, comprehensive, and professionally sound.

4. Develop a Report on the Knowledge Base

Now the Task Force develops a report on the knowledge base for its subject. This report will guide the Task Force's work and provide a basis for staff development. To ensure that the curriculum is based on sound research and practice, Task Force members should search the literature for the following information:

- Research on effective teaching and learning in that subject
- Major national curriculum projects in that field
- The recommendations of experts in that field
- High-quality commercial materials

Several sources can aid this search: the Association for Supervision and Curriculum Development's *ASCD Update* newsletter; *Brown's Directories of Instructional Programs* (also available through ASCD); *ASCD Curriculum Materials Directory*; *ASCD Curriculum Handbook*; ERIC and PsychLit data bases; and professional journals in the field.

The results of the search are then synthesized into a report with three sections:

- Sources of Curricular and Learning Materials
- Recommendations of Experts on Curriculum
- Research on Teaching and Learning

This task might well be assigned to an external consultant with expertise in the subject, since it requires special knowledge retrieval and writing skills. Regardless of who does the report, it also should be reviewed for its quality before it is disseminated.

5. Develop the Hallmarks of Excellence

The "Hallmarks of Excellence" for a given subject are the desirable features of the curriculum in that field of study. In one sense, they constitute a vision for that subject. They are derived from the district vision of curriculum and specify how that general vision will be translated into the desired curriculum attributes for one subject.

To develop the Hallmarks, the Task Force members should review the state framework, the district vision, and the synthesis of the knowledge base. Through open discussion and with timely input from interested teachers, they spell out the Hallmarks that will guide their work.

One useful format indicates in parallel columns what the Task Force members would like to see more of and what they would like to see less of. This design requires them to make productive choices, rather than produce an unrefined grab bag of features. A sample set of Hallmarks for English language arts is shown in Figure 4.1.

6. Develop the Curriculum Framework

The next step is to develop the curriculum framework, which is typically achieved with significant input from administrators, supervisors, and informed teachers. As the term is used here, "curriculum framework" refers to a general description of the chief features of the educational environment and the curriculum to be developed. Thus, it is a set of written statements that address all the following issues that seem relevant:

- For which students is the curriculum being developed? What grade

FIGURE 4.1

Hallmarks of Excellence for English Language Arts

MORE	LESS
1. Language study	1. Grammar
2. Writing for real	2. Themes
3. Content, ideas	3. Spelling, punctuation
4. Literature for meaning	4. Literary terms
5. World classics	5. School classics
6. Culturally diverse	6. Monolithic
7. Mass media	7. Print only
8. Depth	8. Coverage
9. Integrated	9. Fragmented
10. Problem solving and information processing	10. Memorizing

levels are included? What ability ranges?

• Is this curriculum usually implemented as a required subject, an elective, or a combination?

• At the secondary level, is this subject given special names, such as "Biology" or "Chemistry"?

• What total time allocations are recommended for this subject, grade by grade? Is the proposed curriculum designed to occupy all the time allocated, or will it allow for school- or classroom-based enrichment?

• What view of knowledge is represented here? How are the learner and the learning process viewed?

• Will the curriculum attempt to integrate within this field of study (such as a "Unified Science" approach)? Have the possibilities of inter-disciplinary integration been considered?

• Will this curriculum project focus solely on the core or mastery curriculum, or will it include other components?

7. Identify the Strands of the Curriculum

The strands are the components of a field or subject as conceptualized by the developers. They represent the recurring horizontal dimensions of the scope-and-sequence chart. The vertical elements are the grade levels or curriculum levels involved. Here are examples of strands from several subjects, just to clarify the concept:

• English language arts: Writing
• Mathematics: Estimation
• Social studies: Citizenship

Obviously, there is no single correct set of strands for a given curriculum. The best strands are those that seem to meet the following criteria:

• They are conceptually sound; they represent the way that experts in the field conceptualize the field.

• They are teacher-friendly; they are sensitive to how teachers conceptualize the field.

• They are workable; they can be used by developers without a great deal of trouble.

Three major sources should be consulted in developing the strands. First, check to see if the mastery goals classified as "emphasize" can be used as strands. Using the goals as strands is one way to ensure that the subject mastery goals are accomplished. Second, consult the recommendations of state frameworks. Using state-recommended strands may simplify the approval process if the state reviews your guides. Finally, check the strands used by exemplary projects and recommended by professional groups. Many school systems, for example, have found that the standards of the National Council of Teachers of Mathematics can be used as strands in the district curriculum.

Throughout this process, keep in mind (and remind teachers) that the strands are simply a curriculum planning tool, not intended as a structure for teaching. In developing units and teaching students, teachers will often integrate two or more strands.

8. Develop the Scope-and-Sequence Chart

Thus far, the Task Force has developed the mastery goals for a subject, the knowledge base, the Hallmarks of Excellence, the curriculum framework, and the strands. The next major step—and one of the most important—is to develop the scope-and-sequence chart, using all that information and the recommendations of informed classroom teachers.

The process begins by providing staff development for teachers who will be involved in making recommendations for the chart. In smaller districts, this means all elementary teachers and all secondary teachers whose major responsibility is teaching that subject. In larger districts, each school identifies one teacher for each grade level who in turn gets input from team or departmental members.

The staff development should be designed to accomplish the following goals:

- Clarify the concept of the mastery curriculum.
- Clarify the subject mastery goals.
- Review and discuss the knowledge base.
- Review and discuss the Hallmarks of Excellence.
- Clarify the framework.
- Review and discuss the strands.
- Explain the processes by which the scope-and-sequence chart will be developed.

The intent is to develop a cadre of informed teachers who will make specific recommendations for the scope-and-sequence chart, doing so out of a sound and current knowledge of that field.

With staff development completed, the teachers then participate in what is called "mapping for desired mastery."

The Task Force develops the mapping forms to be used, which can be computerized by using optical scannable response forms. The forms should include the following information and directions:

- A brief summary of the knowledge base.
- A note explaining that teachers should recommend what they would like to teach, not what they now teach. The hope is that the staff development and the mapping process will encourage teachers to reach higher than their current practice.
- A reminder that teachers will be asked to recommend only the mastery elements, not organic and enrichment components.
- An explanation that teachers will be asked to recommend only for the grade level they are teaching. Middle school teachers will not tell the elementary teachers what to teach; high school teachers will not dictate to middle school teachers.
- A reminder that teachers should be influenced by their knowledge of child or adolescent development.
- An explanation that the teachers should recommend only the major skills and concepts they wish to teach at that grade level. The scope-and-sequence chart should not be cluttered with detail because it provides a general picture of what will be emphasized. Details will come later, in the curriculum guide.
- A reminder that teachers should recommend for that grade level only those concepts and skills that will be *emphasized* for mastery, not those that will be introduced and reviewed. Again, the intent is to develop an easy-to-read chart, not one cluttered with "I's" (for *introduce*) and "R's" (for *review*). The assumption is that teachers may introduce any concept or skill whenever they feel learners are ready; they should review as necessary, not follow a chart.

- One open page for each strand where teachers will list their recommendations.

Some districts release teachers for a full day of mapping at a central location. Others require each school to hold a special meeting. Whatever the choice, the mapping pages are then submitted to Task Force members, who collate the results and summarize what the teachers have recommended. The resulting chart provides a graphic representation of what teachers believe should be taught for mastery, grade by grade.

Now the Task Forces undertakes the complex task of reviewing teachers' recommendations and making appropriate revisions. In this review, the Task Force will have to address the following issues:

- Are the recommendations professionally sound? Will they enable the district to incorporate high-quality materials from professional groups and national projects?
- Do the recommendations satisfy state requirements and respond adequately to any state tests?
- Do the recommendations respond adequately to any standardized tests that will continue to be used?
- Are the recommendations developmentally sound, reflecting what is known about the cognitive capabilities of students at that grade level?
- Do the recommendations reflect the district vision of curriculum excellence and the Hallmarks of Excellence?
- Do the recommendations sufficiently address the mastery goals of this subject?
- Do the recommendations avoid unnecessary repetition?
- Are the recommendations congruent with the content of any recently adopted textbooks?
- Are the recommendations congruent with any curriculum-referenced tests that will continue to be used?
- Are the recommendations for a given subject generally congruent with the content of existing guides in other closely allied fields of study? This criterion examines the issue of coordination across subjects, ensuring, for example, that the 7th grade science curriculum and the 7th grade mathematics curriculum are closely coordinated.
- Do the recommendations reflect effective articulation from grade to grade in that subject, without excessive repetition?

The Task Force uses the results of this review to develop the first draft of the district's scope-and-sequence chart for the subject under review. The first draft should be submitted for review by teachers, the Citizens Curriculum Advisory Council, the Curriculum Planning Council, and external experts in the field.

If these reviews indicate substantial disagreement on a major issue, the Task Force should then hold open hearings for those interested. It is especially important to involve teachers in such a forum because the intent is to develop a professionally sound curriculum that teachers will support.

Suppose, for example, that many elementary teachers want to teach grammar in grade 5, even though this practice is considered unwise by every expert in the field. The Task Force should meet with these teachers to discuss what is known about child development (5th graders have difficulty learning abstract concepts), what is known about the research (the study of grammar has no practical benefits), and what is provided in other grades (the 7th and 8th grade teachers also want to teach grammar). Through such informed discussion, the 5th grade teachers will know they've been heard, but they will also come to understand why their recommendations have been set aside.

9. Identify Available Curriculum Materials

The developers should next determine if there are professional or commercial curriculum materials already available that can be incorporated (with permission) into the district's curriculum. Note that this decision is made *after* the district has developed its own scope-and-sequence chart. This approach seems better than either ignoring such materials or letting them dictate what teachers must teach.

Locating and incorporating available curriculum materials seems especially useful in science and mathematics, where there is a clear consensus about content and sequence. Several major national projects have developed exemplary units and teaching materials in those subject areas.

If the Task Force locates exemplary materials it wishes to use, members then modify the scope-and-sequence chart accordingly and incorporate the materials into the draft of the curriculum guide.

10. Develop the Curriculum Guide

The Task Force should now turn its attention to the development of the curriculum guide. Some Task Forces turn over this task to a small group of Curriculum Writers; others undertake the task themselves. Obviously, the best time for producing such work is in the summer. My experience leads me to recommend that the writers (whoever they are) be paid by the task, not by the day—and that they not be paid until their work has been reviewed and approved.

What should the curriculum guide include? This is a question that the Curriculum Planning Council should answer. Among the options are:

- The philosophy about curriculum
- The vision of curriculum
- The knowledge base for that subject
- The Hallmarks of Excellence
- The district's educational goals
- The subject mastery goals
- The curriculum framework for the subject
- The scope-and-sequence chart
- The grade-level objectives
- Recommended time allocations
- Recommended sequence for teaching objectives
- Recommended teaching activities for each objective
- Recommended means of assessing student learning
- Textbooks and resources
- Recommendations for fostering organic outcomes
- Recommendations for enriching the curriculum

In resolving this issue, the Planning Council should keep in mind that the goal is to produce a teacher-friendly guide. And, in my experience, there is a negative correlation between the length of the guide and the extent of teacher use. My recommendation, therefore, is that the guide include only these elements:

- The Hallmarks of Excellence
- The subject mastery goals
- The scope-and-sequence chart
- The grade-level objectives

The important issues of sequence of topics and time allocations can better be dealt with at the classroom level.

Also, note that this model does not suggest a teaching/learning activity for each objective. These are omitted for several reasons: they clutter the guide, teachers usually ignore them, and they imply that there is one best activity for each objective. It makes more sense to provide staff development that focuses on effective teaching strategies in that subject. Some districts have decided to include in the guide a summary of the research on such teaching strategies.

The development of the grade-level objectives requires special attention. In general, the best process is for the Curriculum Writers to work one strand at a time for a given grade level. The writer checks the scope-and-sequence entry for that strand and that grade level and analyzes that entry into its component parts, considering the developmental level of the students. The process is a type of task analysis.

Consider, for example, this scope-and-sequence entry for 8th grade social studies:

> Resolving group conflict

The writer considers what specific knowledge and skills are needed to resolve group conflict—and then thinks about what 8th graders can do. The following grade-level objectives would be derived through this process:

- Listen attentively to the views of others.
- Express your own views clearly.
- Identify reasons for disagreement.
- Decide whether to compromise, continue to disagree, or seek additional information.

11. Evaluate the Guide

Two types of evaluation are needed to ensure that the guide is of high quality. The first is a careful study by several groups, using the criteria shown in Figure 4.2 on page 46. The Task Force members responsible for the guide should first make their own evaluations and changes. They should then forward the revised guide to the Planning Council, which should make its own review.

Next, a small group of teachers who will use the guide should review it carefully. Finally, if funds are available, an external expert should make an evaluation focusing on the professional soundness of the materials. Throughout this process, revisions should be made to ensure that the guide is of high quality—reflecting the vision and the Hallmarks, addressing the goals, corresponding with the scope-and-sequence chart, and communicating clearly about grade-level objectives.

The second type of evaluation is through the piloting process. Districts tend to use one of two approaches in testing new curriculums, depending on the resources available. Some implement a focused pilot test. In the focused test, selected teachers in each grade level are asked to use a portion of the guide during the fall semester after the guide has been produced. They implement that portion as best as they can, keep careful notes on their and students' responses, and summarize those views in a systematic report to the Task Force.

Other districts implement a comprehensive pilot test. A representative group of schools is selected to pilot the guide for an entire year. School administrators and teachers are provided with the staff development needed to implement the new guide. Texts and other needed materials are provided. Teachers keep logs noting students' reactions and their own assessments. Close to the end of the school year, curriculum-referenced tests are used to assess student learning.

The extent of curriculum evaluation will vary, obviously, with the resources available and the impact of the new guide. But no guide should be used unless it has been rigorously evaluated in some systematic manner.

FIGURE 4.2

Criteria for Evaluating Curriculum Guides

Format
1. Is the guide easy to use? Is it "teacher friendly"?

Emphases
2. Does the guide make explicit the values that inform it—the view of knowledge that it represents?
3. Does the content of the guide reflect sound research in that field and the recommendations of experts?
4. Does the guide emphasize depth of profound knowledge (instead of coverage), the acquisition of useful skills, and the application of that knowledge and those skills in solving meaningful problems?
5. Do the overall structure and content of the guide reflect and contribute to the district's vision of a curriculum of excellence?
6. Does the guide focus on meaningful outcomes that enable all students to succeed in higher education and develop the requisite career skills?
7. Does the guide develop in students an appreciation of diversity, a valuing of our common heritage, and a concern for equity?

Placement and Sequence
8. Are the grade-level objectives developmentally appropriate?
9. Does the guide provide for a meaningful sequence and coordination of learning, without excessive repetition?

Organization and Structure
10. Does the guide clearly indicate the goals for that subject and how those outcomes relate to the district's educational goals?
11. Are the grade-level objectives derived from subject goals, and are they clearly stated?
12. Does the guide include other materials that teachers have requested, such as learning resources?
13. Does the guide provide for and facilitate the appropriate integration of knowledge within that subject and from related subjects?

12. Determine How the Guide Will Be Distributed

The next major task is deciding which portions of the comprehensive K–12 curriculum guide each classroom teacher should receive. Here are the options:

• Every teacher who teaches the subject receives the complete K–12 guide.

• The teacher receives the components of the guide that relate to the grades included in that school. For example, all middle school science teachers would receive the guide for grades 6–8.

• The teacher receives the guide for his or her grade, as well as that for the grade above and the grade below, regardless of the grade organization pattern used by that school. Thus, a 6th grade middle school science teacher would receive the science guide for grades 5, 6, and 7.

• The teacher receives the guide only for his or her grade.

Most districts find that the third option is a good compromise. It simplifies teachers' use of the guide while giving them some sense of coordination. If a teacher is to receive only a portion of the comprehensive guide, the package should include the subject mastery goals and the entire scope-and-sequence chart.

Renewing the Curriculum

Curriculum renewal is a process of updating and fine-tuning an existing guide. You would renew, rather than develop, a curriculum when your resources are scarce and you are generally satisfied with the existing curriculum but realize that it is a bit out of date. While the process of curriculum renewal has been avoided in all the curriculum texts, it seems from my experience to be a useful process in a time marked by rapid change and scarce resources.

The following steps describe one successful approach to renewal:

1. Review the subject goals to ensure that they are up to date.

2. Update the knowledge base: include current findings that seem important.

3. If necessary, revise the Hallmarks of Excellence. If they were not previously developed, do so now.

4. If necessary, review and revise the framework.

5. Keep the strands of the curriculum previously identified unless you have found them completely unsatisfactory.

6. Revise the scope-and-sequence chart. Using the updated materials, determine whether some entries should be dropped, placed at a different grade level, or added.

7. Use the revised scope-and-sequence chart to revise the grade-level objectives.

8. Submit drafts of the revision to administrators, supervisors, and teachers, revising accordingly. If extensive changes have been made, you should adopt new texts and modify existing curriculum-referenced tests.

5

Supporting the District Curriculum

Too often, district leaders assume that their task is complete once the curriculum guide has been distributed. The results of such a short-sighted attitude are predictable: the new guide is not used. Three important processes are necessary for districts to avoid this problem: aligning the curriculum, producing supporting materials, and monitoring the curriculum.

Aligning the Curriculum

Curriculum alignment can be defined as a process of aligning the written curriculum (the one that appears in guides), the tested curriculum (the one that appears in tests), and the supported curriculum (the one that appears in textbooks and other resources) to make the taught curriculum (the one the teacher actually delivers) more effective.

In the normal sequence of events, texts will be selected and tests developed after the new guide has been produced. In such a case, alignment should be a relatively simple matter. But if you have existing guides you wish to align, the task will be somewhat more complex. In either case, the alignment process accomplishes two related purposes: it serves as a check on guide/text/test congruence, and it provides teachers with an alignment chart that they can use in their own planning.

(Leaders seeking a different perspective on alignment should consult English 1992.)

Organizing for Alignment

In deciding how to organize for alignment, you have three main choices. First, a Task Force may be assigned the job as part of their responsibilities. Or, teachers working in grade-level groups may take charge of the task. You could also use a combination of Task Force and teacher efforts, which is the structure recommended below.

Before any work begins, the Planning Council needs to provide training to ensure that everyone assigned the task of alignment understands the process. The Task Force should then arrange for someone to take the curriculum guide and enter all the objectives into a computer, grade by grade in the order in which they occur in the guide. Next, the Task Force should have all the objectives printed out on a large spreadsheet or chart similar to the sample shown in Figure 5.1.

FIGURE 5.1
Sample Alignment Form

Objectives	Analysis	End-of-Course Test	Standardized Test	Text Pages
1. Identify metaphor	M	X		
2. Listen courteously	O			
3. Use irony	E			

At this point, the grade-level groups take over. Each group is provided with the following materials: the objectives and the chart, materials describing end-of-course tests, any standardized tests used, and copies of basic texts. The teams work together on the following tasks:

1. First, classify the objectives as either *mastery,* *organic,* or *enrichment.* You may recall from Chapter 3 that the mastery objectives have high structure and high importance and require explicit teaching. Organic objectives have high importance but low structure; they should be nurtured in every grade, on every suitable occasion, not assigned to a particular grade level. Enrichment objectives are those that are not really important for all students. As Figure 5.1 shows, use one of these letters to indicate the classification in the column headed "Analysis": M, mastery; O, organic; E, enrichment. If the guide has been produced so that it includes only mastery objectives, this step is not needed.

2. Review the general nature of the end-of-course tests. If a particular objective is likely to be tested, put an X in the "End-of-Course Test" column on the alignment form. If you find an objective likely to be included in the test that is not included in the guide, add it to the list of objectives, code it as "mastery," and put an X in the "End-of-Course Test" column.

3. Review the general nature of the standardized test. If a particular objective is likely to be tested, put an X in the "Standardized Test" column. If you find an objective likely to be included in the standardized test that is not included in the guide, add it to the list of objectives, note it as "mastery," and place an X in the "Standardized Test" column.

4. Analyze the contents of each basic text used in that subject to determine if each objective is adequately treated. If an objective is adequately treated, note in the "Text Pages" column the page numbers of the text where that objective is covered.

Using the Results of Alignment

The results of the work of the grade-level groups should be reviewed by the Task Force and modified if necessary. The Planning Council should do a final review. The results of the alignment process can then be used to guide revisions of and supplements to the guide and also to assist with staff development.

First, the results may indicate that some organic and enrichment objectives have been included in the guide. If so, you should probably revise the guide by including only mastery objectives, using staff development for the organic outcomes, and letting grade-level teams decide how they will handle enrichment objectives. Or you may decide to keep the original guide, simply coding each objective in the guide as mastery, organic, or enrichment.

Second, the results may indicate that some of the mastery objectives in the guide will probably not be tested. Check to be sure that they are in fact mastery outcomes. If they are, remind teachers that they are important, even if they are not likely to be assessed. Consider, for example, this objective: "Listen critically to political speeches." It is a mastery objective that is probably difficult to test, so it won't be. Still, it should be taught.

Also, the alignment results may show that some objectives likely to be tested are not included in the guide. Revise the guide to include those objectives or, if the test has been locally produced, consider revising the test.

The chart may also indicate that some mastery objectives are not treated in the basic texts. This omission suggests that the Task Force should develop or locate supplementary materials that will deal with these objectives. If the text is an old one with little curriculum overlap, consider adopting a new text that is better aligned.

If the alignment process has resulted in some revisions of the guide, then a new chart should be produced reflecting the changes. Finally, the alignment results can also be used to guide staff development. Teachers can use the results in developing mastery-focused units and in working together on enrichment objectives. Teachers will also need help in using the results to develop yearly and unit plans, as explained in Chapter 8.

Producing Supporting Materials

Some districts have seen a need to produce additional materials to aid administrators and teachers. One useful product is an "Observer's Guide" that enables administrators, supervisors, and mentors to make more useful observations of teachers using the new guide. An example of such a guide is shown in Figure 5.2.

Teachers may also be helped by receiving guidelines for fostering organic outcomes. These outcomes are essential, even though they do not have high structure. Figure 5.3 on p. 54 provides an example of a portion of such a guide.

Monitoring the Curriculum

Curriculum monitoring is an evaluation process at the piloting and implementation stages that asks the question "Are teachers implementing the curriculum with reasonable fidelity?" Such monitoring can seem intrusive at times and can imply a distrust of teachers. Thus, it tends to be a matter of great sensitivity among most teachers, and a clear curriculum monitoring policy with accompanying procedures should be established at the district level and carried out uniformly at each school.

Figure 5.2
Observing Social Studies Taught
from a Constructivist Perspective

The following questions are intended to guide observation; they are not a prescriptive checklist.

1. Did the learners seem motivated to learn? Did the teacher seem sensitive to the importance of intrinsic motivation by helping students find meaning and purpose in what was to be learned?

2. Did the learners understand and internalize the learning goal? Was the learning objective relevant, significant, and clear to all?

3. Did the learners activate their prior knowledge? Did the teacher assist in this process and facilitate it?

4. Did the learners acquire new knowledge? Were the means by which they acquired that knowledge the most efficient and effective?

5. Did the learners relate the new knowledge to prior knowledge and modify knowledge constructs accordingly?

6. Did the learners construct personal meaning by organizing, elaborating, and representing knowledge in their own way?

7. Did the learners, with the teacher's help, identify a complex problem to be solved and solve that problem by making knowledge generative?

8. Did the learners seem to have an appropriate amount of scaffolding and structuring from the teacher to solve the problem?

9. Did the learners understand and use the strategies needed to solve the problem? Did the teacher provide the necessary help in this process?

10. Did the learners learn in a supportive social context? Were there reflective dialogue, cooperative inquiry, and the social construction of knowledge?

11. Did the learners use metacognitive monitoring to assess their learning?

12. Did the learners assess their learning and demonstrate their understanding? Did the teacher make periodic assessments of learning and use assessment data to adjust and remediate?

FIGURE 5.3
Fostering Organic Outcomes in Science

The following organic outcomes are important in science. Each should be nurtured on every appropriate occasion. An organic outcome is noted; then several suggestions are offered as means of fostering it.

Develop Scientific Curiosity

1. On the bulletin board, post "puzzlers" that pose intriguing scientific questions.

2. Ask students to look around the classroom and identify questions that could be answered through observation.

3. Display on the bulletin board pictures of scientists who used scientific curiosity to develop successful inventions.

4. Select each week the "Questioner of the Week," a student who asked especially useful questions.

5. Reinforce question asking through appropriate praise.

6. Model scientific curiosity by asking questions that intrigue and interest you.

7. Have students keep a science learning journal in which they record questions they would like to answer.

8. As you introduce a unit, survey students to determine which questions they would like answered.

9. At the end of the unit, help students identify "Unanswered Questions" that still confront scientists.

Some districts decide not to monitor the curriculum, since many teachers resist the process. Those who do monitor use a variety of practices, each of which has advantages and disadvantages.

Analyzing Test Scores

If you have developed valid curriculum-referenced tests, you may decide to monitor implementation by reviewing student performance on those tests. Monitoring by test-score analysis has the advantage of being objective and learning-focused. Its chief disadvantage is the assumption that poor student performance is the result of the teacher's failure to implement the curriculum. Indeed, if students in the classes of a particular teacher consistently perform below expectations, you would undertake a fine-grained item analysis in cooperation with that teacher to pinpoint specific deficiencies.

It should be noted here, however, that formative monitoring of student achievement with the use of computers can be effective. One study by Fuchs and colleagues (1991) concluded that a curriculum-based measurement program that gave teachers feedback about ongoing student achievement was effective in achieving more frequent revision of teachers' plans. When accompanied by "expert system consultation" (a program that reproduced advice that experts might give), this type of monitoring was effective in improving student achievement in mathematics.

Reviewing Teachers' Plans

Some districts choose to monitor by requiring teachers to submit daily or unit lesson plans keyed to the district curriculum guide. The principal reviews the plans to ensure that they sufficiently address the mastery objectives of the guide, conferring with the teacher if necessary. The chief advantage of this approach is that it can facilitate teacher-principal discussions of curriculum. The major drawback is that it assumes that the plans teachers submit are those they actually deliver. Research suggests otherwise.

Reviewing Teachers' Reports

Some districts require teachers to submit weekly reports of what was taught, to determine if the curriculum is being implemented. This is probably the least reliable of all methods, since many teachers will report what they should have taught, not what they actually taught. It also requires a great deal of paperwork for the teacher to produce and the principal to review.

Making Informal Observations in the Classroom

As a regular part of their role, many principals make brief, informal observations of the classroom. During such visits, the principal can systematically observe whether the curriculum is being implemented. Such "drop-in" observations have several advantages:

• They make the principal more visible.

• They provide an opportunity for the principal to affirm effective teaching.

• They can serve as an "early warning system" for instructional problems.

The chief drawback is that these informal visits rely upon a selective sample of teacher behavior. A ten-minute observation will not yield reliable, comprehensive information.

Obviously, no single monitoring system is perfect, but the following approach incorporates the advantages of several and attempts to minimize the drawbacks. It places more emphasis on trust, not inspection.

First, the principal emphasizes a constructive approach throughout the implementation stage, stressing the importance of the new curriculum, ensuring that resources are available, providing the needed staff development, and discussing informally with teachers their reactions to the new curriculum.

Second, the principal systematically analyzes all test scores with the teachers to help them understand poor student performance without implying that any teacher is at fault.

Next, the principal or team leader helps teachers develop effective unit plans based on the curriculum, without using those plans as a means of checking up on teachers (see Chapter 8 for details).

Finally, the principal makes brief, informal classroom visits without relying solely upon those visits as a monitoring process.

6

Ensuring Effective Implementation of the District Guide

In too many districts, a high-quality curriculum guide is written, presented to teachers in a summer workshop, put on a shelf, and then never referred to again.

To avoid such wasted effort, you need to develop and carry out an effective implementation strategy. In fact, as a general rule of thumb, you should allocate more resources to implementing the new curriculum than to developing it. Implementation is a complex change that requires the efforts of all involved if it is to be successful. This chapter describes a current model of effective implementation termed "mutual accomplishment."

The Nature of Mutual Accomplishment

"Mutual accomplishment," a concept introduced by Bird (1986), describes a type of implementation in which the developers of an innovation (in this case, the Curriculum Task Force) accomplish their central goal of changing the curriculum in a positive direction, and the users of the innovation (in this case, the classroom teachers) accomplish their goals of influencing the specifics of the curriculum while retaining their autonomy over daily life in the classroom.

Mutual accomplishment respects the work of the developers while recognizing a continuing need for improvement. It also values districtwide coordination of the central elements of curriculum while acknowledging that each classroom represents a unique context. Mutual accomplishment also honors the professionalism of teachers, valuing their input and granting them the autonomy they need to adapt the curriculum to the demands of their classrooms.

Mutual accomplishment is a sensible midpoint between top-down fidelity and curricular anarchy. Top-down fidelity assumes that the written guide cannot be improved. It must be implemented exactly as the developers formulated it, and teachers simply deliver an externally produced product. Top-down fidelity is not only impossible to achieve, it also devalues the skills of teachers.

Curricular anarchy, on the other hand, is a laissez-faire approach that assumes teachers are curriculum experts. Each classroom is an isolated and self-contained unit in which districtwide curriculum goals are irrelevant and the level of student achievement depends upon the ability of each classroom teacher. The result is a patchwork-quilt curriculum.

The Goals of Mutual Accomplishment

Through the process of mutual accomplishment, educators attempt to achieve the following specific outcomes:

• Teachers plan their work and teach in a manner that accomplishes the objectives of the mastery curriculum as delineated in the curriculum guide.

• Teachers translate those objectives into sound units of study, making appropriate allocations of time and using an effective sequence. They have latitude in making these decisions so they can respond to the special needs of their students.

• Teachers use sound teaching practices in operationalizing the curriculum, but the guide does not prescribe these practices.

• Teachers consistently nurture organic outcomes in a supportive learning environment.

• Teachers develop enrichment units for all students that reflect the teacher's special interests and respond to students' special needs.

• Teachers continually assess student learning and keep careful records of students' problems with the new curriculum. They systematically provide this feedback to the Task Force, and it is used to revise and improve the guide.

Curriculum Support for Mutual Accomplishment

How can the district achieve these goals? According to Fullan's research (1991), four characteristics of an innovation will facilitate effective implementation: the need for change; clarity; complexity; and quality.

The Need for Change

The Task Force should first work with school principals to establish in their minds a need for the new curriculum. In most cases, principals will be persuaded if they are given evidence that the new curriculum will improve student achievement in their school—and that it won't make undue demands on them. They will be less persuaded by arguments such as "the state requires us," "the board wants it," "the National Council of Teachers of Mathematics recommends it," or, "the research says."

Principals, in turn, can then work with their teachers to establish a similar awareness of need. In doing so, they should keep in mind that, at this stage, teachers usually want information about the new curriculum—its general characteristics, its goals, and its requirements for teaching. (See Loucks-Horsley and Stiegelbauer 1991 for research on teachers' concerns at varying stages of implementation.)

Clarity

Clarity is critical in two respects. First, the curriculum guide itself must be clear. This is accomplished by providing an uncluttered scope-and-sequence chart that indicates only major concepts and skills and notes the grade level for primary emphasis. The guide must focus on the mastery objectives without many extraneous details, and those objectives should be expressed in plain, specific language.

Clarity is also needed in communicating about the new curriculum guide to administrators, teachers, parents, and students. The Hallmarks of Excellence should be a useful beginning point for such dialogue, so long as they are free of educational jargon and vague slogans. Contrast these two examples:

Unsatisfactory: Our new science guide is based on constructivist principles and embraces a learning styles approach.

Better: Our new science guide has the learner acquire science knowledge and then use that knowledge in solving real problems. It encourages teachers to vary the methods of instruction so all students can understand the concepts and master the skills.

Complexity

According to research, complex changes have little chance of being implemented effectively unless they are introduced incrementally. This finding is illustrated in the failure of the complex "teacher-proof" curriculums developed in the 1960s. Such curriculums required teachers to acquire the sophisticated knowledge of experts in the field and assumed that such knowledge could be gained and internalized in a few staff development sessions on "the new math" or "transformational grammar."

The first place to avoid excess complexity is the curriculum guide itself. An unduly complex guide expects the teacher to use too many resources, to keep in mind too many curriculum elements at the same time, and to accomplish too many difficult goals. Developers will avoid this problem if they keep in mind the audience for whom they are writing (3rd grade teachers are not experts in science), test the guide in a systematic piloting process, and solicit teacher input in revising the guide.

Perhaps a more important need is to offer teachers ongoing support through staff development programs. These programs need to be planned so that they respond to teachers' emerging needs with the new curriculum and do not overwhelm them with too much information at once. Figure 6.1 shows part of the schedule for a needs-responsive program that helps teachers implement a complex curriculum. Notice that the summer institute provides teachers with enough information and training to get off to a good start. The rest of the program identifies the needs that teachers will have early in the implementation process and provides specific time for teachers to identify and work together on emerging problems.

Quality

The quality of an innovation is also an influential factor. If school administrators perceive the new guide to be of high quality, they will be more inclined to support its implementation. If teachers have the same perception, they are more likely to use it. As emphasized throughout this book, high quality should be ensured throughout the entire curriculum development process and at all levels of curriculum work.

Curriculum quality is achieved by focusing on mastery objectives only, reducing the scope of coverage, explicitly providing for and supporting the development of enrichment units, and giving teachers autonomy with respect to pacing and instructional strategies. This approach embodies a vision of teachers as active collaborators in the curriculum process, not mindless implementers.

At the same time, the Task Force should work with principals to take the steps needed to provide quality instructional materials in timely fashion. Teachers are often frustrated in implementing a new guide when they discover that new materials have not arrived.

Figure 6.1
Sample Staff Development Plan

Focus: Implementing the New Science Curriculum
Audience: K–5 teachers

Summer Institute
Getting started with the new science curriculum:
* Understanding its Hallmarks of Excellence and the view of knowledge that it reflects
* Using the new texts
* Developing yearly plans
* Planning for the first few weeks

September
Developing and maintaining a supportive learning environment. Managing active groups.

October
Using hands-on materials for meaningful learning. Identifying and responding to emerging problems.

November
Assessing student learning and using student errors in developing new concepts. Identifying and responding to emerging problems.

The District's Role in Mutual Accomplishment

The district has five important roles in helping achieve mutual accomplishment: effective planning for implementation, administrative support, staff development, evaluation, and board and community support.

Effective Planning for Implementation

The Task Force that developed the curriculum should be responsible for creating an implementation calendar that reflects a systematic but flexible plan for using the new curriculum. With input from district supervisors, school administrators, and representative teachers, the Task Force should identify the key steps to be taken, the target dates for each step, and the individual or group responsible. In my experience, a modified Gantt chart has been successful for organizing this information. Down the left side, list these planning elements:

- Guide production and distribution
- Materials acquisition
- Staff development for school administrators
- Staff development for teachers
- Evaluation and feedback

Across the top, list the time periods for the implementation stage, usually expressed in two-week increments. In the columns below, indicate each specific step along with the person or group responsible.

The planning calendar should be reviewed and revised periodically as teachers use the guide and principals make their evaluations. Such "evolutionary planning," as Fullan (1991) terms it, is more effective than a tight, inflexible schedule.

Administrative Support

The superintendent, the assistant superintendent for curriculum, and the appropriate central office supervisors should also emphasize their strong support for the curriculum. In too many instances, the superintendent assumes that his or her support is understood and neglects to make it explicit. Teachers often interpret silence as indifference.

Central office personnel should make their strong support clear in speaking, writing, and actions. Praising the task force for its work, emphasizing the need for the new curriculum, stressing the expectation that it will be implemented, and being open to principals' and teachers' concerns—all these actions are needed. More important, of course, is support that is translated into action: providing needed materials, planning and carrying out effective staff development programs, and fostering a supportive climate that recognizes the difficulties of implementing a new curriculum.

Staff Development

As noted above, ongoing staff development is needed for both school administrators and teachers. Principals and assistant principals need to understand the special roles they play in this process, as noted in Chapter 7. Teachers also need the continuing support provided by staff development programs that respond to their emerging problems.

As outlined in Chapters 3 and 4, teacher involvement in the curriculum development process is also essential if they are to support the new curriculum and implement it effectively.

Evaluation

A systematic process for ongoing evaluation is essential for ensuring quality. First, all products should be evaluated carefully and revised accordingly: the district's educational goals, its vision of curriculum excellence, the scope-and-sequence chart, and the written curriculum guide. Second, as noted in Chapter 4, the new guide should be pilot-tested to assess its feasibility and perceived effectiveness.

Next, evaluation processes should be built into the implementation plan. As teachers use the guide with students, they should note and report both successes and problems. As principals monitor the implementation, they should systematically report their observations, too. Finally, the effects of the guide should be measured through the evaluation of student performance on curriculum-referenced tests. All this information from teachers, principals, and students can be used to revise the guide so that it reflects the knowledge gained through actual implementation.

Board and Community Support

As Fullan (1991) notes, any innovation is more likely to be implemented successfully if it enjoys board support and if it does not provoke community controversy. The superintendent needs to keep the board briefed about the need for and nature of the new curriculum, providing board members with enough information to understand it and interpret it to the community. The Citizens Curriculum Advisory Council can play an active role in alerting both the board and the Curriculum Planning Council to any areas of potential controversy. The Advisory Council can also recommend strategies in two areas: (1) responding to potential areas of conflict and misunderstanding and (2) developing support for the new curriculum in the community.

The School's Role in Mutual Accomplishment

Research indicates that three school-level factors are crucial to mutual accomplishment: the role of the principal, teacher-teacher relationships, and teacher attitudes.

The Role of the Principal

The principal plays a critical role in facilitating effective implementation, as detailed further in Chapter 7. Effective professional development can help the principal provide leadership in the implementation stage. Such professional development would encompass the following knowledge and skills:

- The need for the new curriculum
- Hallmarks of Excellence of the new curriculum
- Teaching changes required by the new curriculum
- Observing the new curriculum in action
- Monitoring the implementation of the new curriculum
- Supporting teachers during the implementation stage
- Evaluating the new curriculum

Teacher-Teacher Relationships

According to Fullan's review of research, the more that teachers cooperate in implementing the guide, the more effective the implementation will be. As noted in a previous work (Glatthorn 1990), such collaboration can be effectively achieved through a process termed *cooperative development* in which small teams of teachers work together, as an alternative to clinical supervision. At the elementary and middle school levels, such teams will probably be organized according to grade level; at the high school, according to department.

The following cooperative development activities support effective implementation:

• Developing yearly calendars for teaching the new curriculum,
• Developing units of study based on the new curriculum,
• Developing enrichment units for the curriculum,
• Holding peer observations and conferences focusing on colleagues' implementation of the curriculum,
• Exchanging ideas for fostering the organic curriculum,
• Identifying and solving problems with the new curriculum, and
• Evaluating the new curriculum and developing a comprehensive feedback report to the Task Force

Teacher Attitudes

Finally, the Task Force, district administrators, school administrators, and other colleagues need to work together to foster an attitude of change among teachers so they feel intrinsically motivated to implement the new curriculum effectively. Four teacher attitudes seem essential:

• I welcome curriculum change as an organizational need and as a stimulus for my own growth.
• I believe in the new curriculum as a means of fostering student achievement.
• I believe in my ability to implement the new curriculum and achieve positive results with it.
• I am a professional whose skills and knowledge are respected, and I can influence the development and revision of the curriculum.

This attitude change can be difficult to accomplish, since teachers' predispositions are often deeply entrenched. But the task is not impossible. Research suggests that attitude change can be accomplished under the following circumstances. First, administrators, supervisors, and key colleagues affirm the desired attitudes as being professionally desirable. Second, teachers receive the training and support they need to implement the new curriculum effectively. Third, leaders and trainers understand and value teachers' concerns. Next, administrators put appropriate pressure on teachers to implement the new curriculum and to assess its effects. Finally, teachers are rewarded for changing attitudes and behaviors. Note that the strategies in some part reflect the findings of Huberman and Miles (1986) that commitment to an innovation, rather than being a necessary antecedent to change, often results from putting the innovation into practice and seeing its effects.

7

Developing the School Curriculum

As noted previously, one key assumption of this book is that school-based curriculum development should operate within the parameters of the district's curriculum to ensure equity and coordination across the district. Not all advocates of school-based decision making would agree, of course. Bailey (1991), for example, would place more curriculum control at the school level. Obviously the issue is an important one for district and school leaders to resolve as they move toward school-based decision making.

Yet the assumption that school-based planning should operate within the district's limits does not mean that school leaders have no role in curriculum development. In fact, they play a very active part in developing a special curriculum for their school within district constraints. Regardless of the committee structure used for curriculum work at the school, there will be a need for strong leadership, which is typically provided by the principal. (In some schools, however, the assistant principal or another individual will assume major responsibility for curriculum leadership.) And in every case, teacher leaders will be actively involved in the process.

Leadership Tasks at the School Level

If district leadership has accomplished the tasks explained in the previous chapter, what is left for school-based leadership?[*]

1. Developing a Culture That Supports Curriculum Work. The principal provides leadership in developing and maintaining a culture that supports curriculum work. By using the reward system judiciously, demonstrating a concern about curriculum, and stressing the importance of teachers' curriculum work, the principal nurtures the values and norms of collegiality, teamwork, and continuous improvement, especially with respect to curriculum. By talking about curriculum, stressing its importance, and speaking knowledgeably about general curriculum matters, the principal encourages teachers to value curriculum work.

2. Providing Support for Curriculum Work. The principal also takes leadership in ensuring that teachers' curriculum work gets the necessary support. First there is a need for a supportive climate during the implementation of new curriculums, when teachers often experience special problems. The principal encourages teachers to take risks, reduces the pressure of teacher evaluation during early implementation, and encourages teachers to identify problems with the new curriculum.

Support also involves providing quality time to enable teachers to develop the materials they will need to implement the curriculum effectively (such as yearly planning calendars, sample units, and instructional materials). While instructional time needs to be defended, the principal also must understand the importance of providing special time devoted to curriculum work. Teams and departments should be encouraged to use planning time for developing curriculum units and learning materials.

This support function also means ensuring that the learning materials needed to implement the curriculum are available. Teachers are often frustrated because needed materials are not on hand. The principal is probably in the best position to ensure that materials arrive in timely fashion and to pressure the business office to respond to any problems.

Also, the principal supports the curriculum by working with teachers in planning and implementing the staff development needed to support implementation. In general, district leaders should train principals to lead school-based staff development rather than rely on districtwide sessions.

---

[*]The following sources were useful in this analysis: Berlin, Kavanagh, and Jensen 1988; Murphy 1990; and Griffin 1988.

Support also includes facilitating the technical support teachers need in implementing new curriculums. Although the principal is not expected to be an expert in all areas of the curriculum, he or she should know where and how to get help—from central office staff, from professors in area universities, and from curriculum consultants.

3. Performing Evaluation Functions. Several critical evaluation functions require the leadership of the principal. First, the program of studies for the school needs to be evaluated. This evaluation is a process of examining the entire set of offerings at a given level of schooling to ensure the program meets certain specified standards, such as providing a quality education for all students, regardless of ability, and developing the special interests and talents of students. Specific suggestions for evaluating the program of studies can be found below.

Second, the principal should be active in monitoring the implementation of curriculums. While the school district typically will develop a district monitoring plan, the principal should ensure that the curriculum in that school is effectively implemented. (The recommended methods for monitoring the curriculum were explained in Chapter 6.)

Also, the principal should play an active role in evaluating the effectiveness of new curriculums. While the district should develop a comprehensive program for evaluating the effectiveness of new curriculums, the principal is in a key position to provide evaluation data. By conferring with teachers, talking with students, reviewing test and other performance results, and observing classes, the principal can become aware of developing problems and emerging strengths.

Another key evaluation function is assessing the coordination between levels of schooling. If curriculum Task Forces have done their job effectively, there should be a well-coordinated K–12 program where learning is unaffected by the divisions between levels of schooling. Such coordination is so essential, however, that the principal should play an active role in assessing whether discontinuities are occurring from level to level. By analyzing test scores, conferring with classroom teachers, and discussing the issue with the principals of sending and receiving schools, the principal is in a special position to detect problems of level-to-level coordination.

Leadership is also required in assessing whether the hidden curriculum is congruent with the espoused values of the administrators and teachers. Here the principal and teachers need to systematically examine the impact of such elements as the reward system, the disciplinary policies, the physical environment, and the allocation of funds.

Finally, the principal can lead by assessing the extent to which the several curriculums are aligned. As explained previously, curriculum alignment is a process of ensuring that the supported curriculum of texts and other materials and the tested curriculum are congruent with the written curriculum. Alignment strengthens the taught curriculum.

All these processes will require that the principal become generally knowledgeable about:

- Major national developments in the general area of curriculum
- General curriculum trends in each subject area
- Significant features of new curriculums to be implemented
- Methods for observing the effective implementation of curriculums

4. Developing School Goals and Vision. The first task of the School Curriculum Council is to determine if the school should have its own set of goals and its own vision of curriculum. It is probably desirable for the school to supplement the district's foundation documents; doing so gives the faculty a sense of their school's uniqueness while enabling them to support the district's outcomes and vision. Such a supplement would be especially important in a magnet school that has a special curriculum emphasis.

The process begins when all teachers meet to discuss the district's goals, focusing on these related issues:

- Do the district's goals respond appropriately to the special nature of our school?
- Do the district's goals reflect the special nature of the community we serve?
- Do the district's goals respond appropriately to the special needs of our students?

After this discussion, the faculty may decide to add a goal, to give special emphasis to one or more goals, or to append a general statement to the district's goal statement. An example of one such document is shown in Figure 7.1 on page 70.

With the goal statement produced, the Council next turns to the vision statement. If the curriculum development process described in this book has been followed, then faculty members have already prepared a vision of a curriculum of excellence, and the Council simply needs to review the vision statement to be sure that it still represents what the school hopes to achieve. If this process has not been followed, a vision statement can be developed at this juncture. (As noted in Chapter 3, the faculty should always review the goal and vision statements from time to time.)

FIGURE 7.1
A School's Goal Statement

The administrators and teachers of the Fairway Middle School, a Science Magnet school, endorse strongly the goals of the Washington School District. In addition we commit ourselves to the following beliefs and practices with respect to our curriculum.

First, we will give special attention to the developmental needs of our middle school students as we work towards the accomplishment of the district's goals. In this sense we will pay special attention to their social and emotional needs as they work through the stage of early adolescence.

Second, given our emphasis on science, we will give focused attention to developing scientific curiosity, to nurturing scientific creativity, and to using scientific knowledge to solve community problems.

Preliminary Steps in Program Review

Given the current interest in school-based management and the importance of having a program that teachers feel some ownership of, each school should develop its own program of studies, working within guidelines provided by the Curriculum Planning Council and using its own version of the process detailed here:

1. Set the District's Limits. At the outset of a review of the program of studies, the Curriculum Planning Council should develop with teacher, supervisor, and administrator input specific guidelines that set the parameters for the schools' programs of study. The guidelines should address the following issues:

• Are there certain subjects that must be studied by all students?

• Are there constraints governing how many and which electives will be offered?

• Are there restrictions governing time allocated and credits awarded?

• Is there a district promotion/graduation/retention policy that must be observed?

• Is there a district policy concerning ability grouping and tracking?

• Are there restrictions concerning the extracurricular activities that may be made available to students?

• By what review process is a school's proposed program formally adopted?

2. Decide Whether to Renew or Restructure. With the limits in place, each school faculty should decide whether it wishes to renew or restructure its program of studies. *Renew* is used here in the sense of making fine adjustments and minor modifications to the existing program of studies. *Restructure* refers to a radical reconceptualization of the program of studies, resulting in a completely new program.

Renewing the program of studies can probably be accomplished in one year; restructuring a program would most likely require three or more years. Both processes are explained in this chapter. Each should be accomplished under the direction of the School Curriculum Council, which gets input from and submits its recommendations to the faculty. In deciding whether to renew or restructure, each school should consider the quality of its present program, the extent of faculty interest, the support of parents, the needs of students, and the resources available.

3. Decide How Many Different Programs Will Be Developed. The School Council next must determine whether each grade will have a different program or whether a single program of studies will be offered at all grades. It also must decide whether special curriculum tracks will be organized into different programs of study. For example, the current interest in vocational/technical programs has led some high schools to offer two programs of study, one for students who anticipate attending a four-year college and one for students with a vocational orientation (For practical suggestions for teaching generic work-related skills in both academic and vocational classrooms, see Stasz and colleagues 1993). The process described here can be used in renewing or restructuring any given program of study.

Renewing the School's Program of Studies

When you renew your school's program of studies, you evaluate and revise the entire set of educational offerings, considering such questions as these:

- Should we give more time to science in the primary grades?
- Does our middle school curriculum respond to the special needs of young adolescents?
- Should we increase high school graduation requirements?

Obviously, many of these program issues have already been resolved for you. Your state has probably specified minimum time allocations for the various subjects. Your local board may have adopted curriculum policies delineating high school graduation requirements. And the K–12 curriculum guides in the different subject-matter areas implemented throughout the district control much of what is offered in a particular school. Despite the number of policies and guides, you still have some latitude in shaping the program of studies for a given level of schooling or for a particular school.

Should each school at a particular level have its own individual program of studies or should all schools at that level have essentially the same program? This is obviously an important matter for boards and superintendents to decide. There are strong arguments for uniform programs in all schools at a particular level. Uniformity results in greater efficiency and probably a more equitable allocation of resources. And it is less likely that parents and the general public will make invidious comparisons between the schools. On the other hand, there are good reasons for giving individual schools some latitude in shaping their own programs. Some research suggests that principals and teachers have a stronger commitment to their school's program of studies when they have had a considerable amount of influence in determining its nature. (For a cogent argument in support of school-based curriculum development, see Bailey 1991.) And school-generated programs would seem more likely to respond to the special needs of the students of that school.

A reasonable resolution of this dilemma would be for district leaders to require all schools to accomplish the district's educational goals, provide a uniform per-pupil budget for all schools at a particular level, and then give each school wide latitude in determining how it will achieve those goals for its pupils. The discussion that follows, then, assumes that schools have some latitude in determining their program of studies; however, the same basic process could be used on a districtwide basis.

Preliminary Steps in the Renewal Process

First, secure the necessary approval and establish needed mechanisms. Let the superintendent know that you intend to assess and improve the program of studies; assure him or her that no major changes will be made without going through appropriate channels. Use the School Curriculum Council (or some analogous group) to direct the project.

Next, identify the evaluation criteria. There are several sources you can use in determining the criteria to be used. Most accrediting bodies specify criteria and standards that the program of studies should meet. Books and articles on restructuring schools also may include criteria for assessing the program of studies (see, for example, Murphy 1991). The

Council may want to review the criteria in Figure 7.2 to determine if they adequately address the issues local educators believe are important. These criteria have been developed by reviewing the current literature on curriculum, by analyzing the criteria of accrediting bodies, and by reflecting on my own experience in helping schools improve their programs. (The criteria are intended to be free of any ideological bias, although they undoubtedly reflect my own view of educational issues.) The faculty should consider the criteria in Figure 7.2 as suggestions only, modifying them as they see fit.

Next, use the criteria to develop an assessment and improvement agenda. By reflecting on the criteria and by analyzing the present program of studies, the Council members should identify criteria that seem to have special relevance for their school. Because these criteria deal with far-reaching issues and involve time-consuming processes, it makes sense to focus the improvement effort on two or three of the criteria that seem most critical. As will be explained shortly, most of the assessments require extensive faculty involvement, and most faculty have only limited tolerance for program improvement efforts.

FIGURE 7.2
Criteria for Evaluating a Program of Studies

A sound program of studies is . . .

1. GOAL-ORIENTED. The program of studies enables the students to accomplish the district's mastery goals.

2. BALANCED. The program of studies provides an appropriate balance between required courses that ensure mastery of essential knowledge and skills and elective courses that enable students to develop and pursue special interests; and the time allocated to those subjects appropriately reflects the school's curricular priorities.

3. INTEGRATED. The program of studies enables students to understand the interrelationship of knowledge and to use knowledge from several disciplines to examine personal and societal problems.

4. SKILLS-REINFORCED. The skills required for learning in many subject areas (writing to learn, reading in the content areas, critical thinking, and learning and studying skills) are given appropriate and timely emphasis.

5. OPEN-ENDED. The program of studies gives all students the knowledge and skills they may need for future success: Students are not tracked into dead-end programs on the basis of premature career choices.

6. RESPONSIVE. The program of studies is responsive to the special needs of the student population served by that school.

The Council should then develop a detailed implementation calendar, showing for each criterion the steps to be taken and the targeted completion dates. The steps to be taken are explained in the next section of this chapter ("Assessing for Renewal"); the dates can be determined by assessing the readiness of the faculty and the resources available. This proposed implementation schedule should then be reviewed by school and district leadership.

Finally, the Council should provide continuing leadership in implementing the procedures and keeping administrators and teachers informed about progress and problems.

Assessing for Renewal

With preliminary matters resolved, the Council turns to the issues it has decided to assess and improve. Below, you'll find a brief explanation of the criteria listed in Figure 7.2 along with a recommended assessment process for each.

Criterion 1: A Sound Program of Studies Is Goal-Oriented. Since the program of studies is the chief mechanism by which the students accomplish the district's mastery goals, the assessment process should determine to what extent the school's program of studies is consonant with the district's goals. Some evidence indicates that schools are more effective when goals and curriculums are aligned (see, for example, Wang, Haertel, and Walberg 1990).

If the Curriculum Planning Council has used the process explained in Chapter 5 to align district goals and the curriculum, then you need only provide the kinds of support explained above to help teachers focus on learning goals. If your district has not aligned goals and curriculum, then the following school-based process should work (the school-based process is a slight modification of the district process).

First, the School Council should identify the school's educational goals. They then should allocate those educational goals to the several programs, such as the mastery curriculum and the activity program. They then should ask each subject team to indicate which of those mastery goals it will emphasize and reinforce. The Council should review the results to ensure that all the mastery goals are being emphasized in at least one subject and that certain goals involving more than one subject are suitably reinforced. If the Council finds serious gaps, then discussions with the appropriate subject teams are held.

The subject teams then focus on the mastery goals they will emphasize or reinforce. For each, they note the specific course or grade level where that goal will be achieved. They then identify the specific units in each course or at each grade level that emphasize or reinforce each goal. The team submits a report to the School Council summarizing these decisions.

The Council then collates and examines all these subject reports, checking to ensure that each goal is suitably emphasized, that there is not undue repetition, and that opportunities for correlation and integration are noted.

Criterion 2. A Sound Program of Studies Is Balanced. The program of studies should provide an appropriate balance between required courses that ensure mastery of essential knowledge and skills and elective courses that enable students to develop and pursue special interests; the time allocated to those subjects should appropriately reflect the school's curriculum priorities.

This criterion is perhaps the most difficult of all to apply, for it involves subjective judgments about what constitutes "appropriate balance" and which subjects are most important. Predictably, there are sharp differences of opinion here. On the one hand, educators such as Theodore Sizer advocate a sharply focused curriculum that gives sole attention to the intellectual dimension of schooling. His prospectus for the "Coalition of Essential Schools" (1985) puts the matter this way:

> The schools should focus on helping adolescents to learn to use their minds well. Schools should not attempt to be "comprehensive" if such a claim is made at the expense of the school's central intellectual purpose. . . . The school's goals should be simple: that each student master a limited number of essential skills and areas of knowledge (p. 2).

At the same time, a large number of teachers and parents believe schools should offer a comprehensive and diversified program. Consider the evidence from John Goodlad's (1984) survey of parents. Goodlad and his researchers asked parents how they would rate these four types of goals: intellectual, vocational, personal, and social. Their response was clear and direct: All four types of goals are "very important." Goodlad summed up the results this way: "We want it all."

Even the research is somewhat inconclusive. First, two scholars who carried out a retrospective analysis of transcripts and college entrance test scores found that students who completed the "new basics" (the more rigorous academic curriculum recommended by several reform reports) had considerably higher test scores than those who did not (Alexander and Pallas 1983). And Lee, Bryk, and Smith (1993) conclude on the basis of their review that "student course taking and tracking are the most powerful predictors of academic achievement . . . " (p. 217). On the other hand, Mora and Kearney (1991) found that increases in the number of mathematics and English language arts courses were not accompanied by improved achievement. And my own (Glatthorn 1986a) review of the evidence suggests that an academically rigorous curriculum might unduly penalize at-risk youth.

The research is generally consistent, however, in underscoring the direct relation between time allocated to a particular subject and achievement in that subject: The more time you allocate to a subject, the higher the achievement level (see, for example, Walberg 1988).

In the end, you have to rely on the limited research available, your own experience, your analysis of the needs of the students in the school, and your assessment of faculty and parent preferences. Here is a relatively simple but effective way of accomplishing the task.

First, prepare a chart like the one shown in Figure 7.3. Then decide how you will indicate time allocations: minutes each week, hours each week or total hours for the year, instructional periods each week, units

FIGURE 7.3
Time Allocations for All Subjects

Subject	Minimum Requirements	Requirements Recommended by Experts	Our Present Requirements	Our Desired Requirements
English, Language Arts, Reading				
Social Studies				
Mathematics				
Science				
Foreign Language				
Health/ Physical Education				
Arts				
Other				
Total Requirements				
Electives				

of credit, or percentage of total instructional time available. Use a time allocation that will best help the teachers assess balance. The recommendation here is to report the number of 45-minute instructional periods for each week, although elementary teachers tend not think about "periods." The important point is to be consistent and clear about how you indicate time allocations.

Then note on the chart the minimum requirements established by the state or the local district. Those entries will remind you and the teachers of the operating limits within which you will have to work. Then report what the experts recommend. To simplify this task, Figure 7.4 lists Goodlad's (1984) elementary recommendations, my own recommendations for the middle grades, and Boyer's (1983) recommendations for the high school. You may, of course, consult other expert sources; the point is to let the teachers know how some educational leaders have interpreted the issue of balance.

Then note on the chart your present time allocations. Now you have three sets of data displayed side by side: required minimums, recom-

FIGURE 7.4
Recommended Time Allocations

Subject	Grades 1–4	Grades 5–8	Grades 9–12
English Language Arts, Reading	10	6	5 (for 2½ years)
Social Studies	3	5	5 (for 3½ years)
Mathematics	7	5	5 (for 2 years)
Science	3	5	5 (for 2 years)
Foreign Language	–	–	2 (for 1 year)
Health/Physical Education	3	3	2 (for 1 year)
Arts	5	3	2 (for 1 year)
Technology	–	–	2 (for 1 year)
Seminar on Work	–	–	2 (for 1 year)
Senior Independent Project	–	–	2 (for 1 year)
Electives	2	2	16 (average each year)
Total Periods	33	35	35

mended allocations, and present requirements. Leave the "desired requirements" column blank; you will complete that later.

Next, use the information on the chart as the basis for organized discussions with faculty and parents. Point out that time is a limited resource and that time allocations seem directly related to achievement. Then ask the questions reflected in the criterion: Does our present program of studies have the desired balance between requirements and electives, and do our time allocations reflect our educational priorities? That general issue subsumes these specific questions:

- Are we giving enough time to the basic academic subjects?
- Are we giving enough time to subjects that nurture the aesthetic and the creative development of the learner?
- Are we giving enough time to subjects that nurture the health and physical development of the learner?
- Are we giving enough time to subjects that will prepare students for the world of work?
- Does the program of studies provide the desired balance between required subjects and electives? Is there enough time for electives that develop special interests and talents?

At the end of the discussion, ask everyone present to complete the last column on the chart, which asks for recommendations for the "desired" requirements. Then analyze the responses on the chart and reflect on the discussions to determine whether there is strong support for any particular change. As you consider the options (lengthening the school day, increasing time allotments to a particular subject, adding a subject, or changing the balance between required and elective courses), remember that major changes of this sort will have a significant impact on staff and budget.

If there is general agreement that students need more choices, consider whether *content options* might be useful. The term is used here to identify content choices within a required discipline or subject matter, to distinguish this kind of choice from deciding whether or not to take a subject. Content-option electives were popular during the early 1970s as 9- or 12-week mini-courses. Thus, instead of taking English I, a student could choose from an array of courses with titles such as *African-American Literature, Hispanic Voices,* and *Women in Literature.* Although such content-option choices were widely criticized as having contributed to the decline in SAT scores (see Cooperman 1978, for example), they were never subjected to a rigorous evaluation. It is quite likely that whatever weaknesses they did have were a result of careless design.

It would seem especially appropriate to consider content options for students in grades 7 to 10. Elementary teachers can provide content options in their self-contained classrooms without any fuss at all; and students in grades 11 and 12 preparing for college and a career probably need carefully structured courses that control content.

Criterion 3. A Sound Program of Studies Is Articulated, Coordinated, and Appropriately Integrated. This criterion focuses on curriculum connections. *Articulation* is used here to mean the linkages from grade to grade and level to level. Since articulation should be the central concern of district Task Forces as they develop subject-specific curriculum guides, the assessment of articulation can focus on the implementation of the curriculums. The analysis of test results and discussions with teachers can help you determine if there are serious gaps or undue repetition from grade to grade.

Coordination is used here to mean the linkages between subjects at a particular grade level. You determine, for example, whether 7th grade science and 7th grade mathematics suitably reinforce each other. The problem of lack of coordination is most acute at the high school level. Elementary teachers in self-contained classrooms do their own informal coordination, and grade-level teams in middle schools focus on coordination issues as they do their planning. In high school, however, departmentalization often creates problems of coordination.

One simple way to assess coordination is to assemble academic teachers at a particular grade level and ask them to put their yearly schedules side by side to compare them. Such an across-subject comparison will suggest some adjustments that can result in better articulation: altering the sequence of units, developing integrated units, adding content to a particular subject, or notifying the Curriculum Planning Council of serious discontinuities.

Integration is the use of several approaches that link the subjects with one another to help students understand the interrelationship of knowledge and to use knowledge from several disciplines to examine personal and societal problems. The extent to which integration should be used is one of the perennial issues that divide the conservatives and liberals. The conservatives argue for the integrity of the disciplines: English is English, and social science is social science; they should not be mixed together. Liberals respond by attacking "curricular fragmentation" and the "curriculum patchwork quilt." What is needed in the debate is enlightened deliberation, not sloganeering.

Chapter 8 reviews the arguments about, and the evidence for, integration. In general, research suggests that you may safely experiment with integrated courses as long as you maintain a focus on essential skills and knowledge, achieving an appropriate balance between integrated and subject-focused experiences. What is an appropriate balance? That key issue, of course, should be resolved at the local level. Chapter 8 provides some general guidelines you can use to resolve this matter.

Criterion 4. A Sound Program of Studies Is Skills-Reinforced. This criterion examines whether the skills required for learning in many subject areas are given appropriate and timely emphasis. In a sound program of studies, separate subjects are strongly laced together with the key learning skills that cut across disciplines. All of the skills required for learning in many areas are given appropriate and timely emphasis. There seem to be four crucial sets of skills: writing to learn; reading in the content areas; critical thinking and problem solving; and learning and studying skills (including information processing). Because by their very nature these skills often fall in the cracks between the subject fields ("it's not my job to teach study skills"), the need to teach and reinforce them seems especially acute at the middle and high school levels, where the cracks are widest of all. On the other hand, in some schools there is undue repetition from subject to subject. For example, both the history teacher and the English teacher may teach the term paper—with different requirements as to style and format.

The following approach seems to be effective in ensuring the mastery of skills across the disciplines without excessive repetition (writing to learn is used as the example).

First, the leaders should determine whether one specific subject will have primary responsibility for teaching the foundational components— those aspects of the skill that seem to apply to several disciplines. For example, by examining the English curriculum guide, the leaders determine that all English teachers should teach the essential components of academic writing that apply to all disciplines, such as documenting sources appropriately. All departments are informed about the foundational skills that will be taught in this primary subject.

Then each departmental team is asked to indicate which of these alternatives it desires to select with respect to this issue:

• We will reinforce this skill by using it systematically and by drawing upon the foundational elements. For example, teachers of home economics may decide to use writing systematically, simply relying upon the foundational skills.

• We will reinforce this skill by using it systematically, but we will also build upon that foundation by adding our own special skills. For example, the social studies department might wish to add the skill of using primary sources in the social sciences.

• We do not plan to reinforce or make systematic use of this skill in this subject. For example, the teachers of physical education may sensibly decide that they will not use writing as a means of helping students develop motor skills.

The Curriculum Council should then review those recommendations, consult with teams whose decisions they question, and develop a preliminary draft of a schoolwide chart showing where the foundational skills are taught and where they are reinforced. The entire faculty should then review the results to be sure that they understand and support the decisions reflected in the chart. The Council then follows up by helping teachers develop the materials needed to teach the foundation skills in one subject and the subject-specific skills in others.

Criterion 5. A Sound Program of Studies Is Open-Ended. This criterion assesses whether the program of studies gives all students the knowledge and skills they may need for future success. In examining this issue, it is important to distinguish between *ability grouping* and *curriculum tracking,* a distinction often overlooked by many critics. Ability grouping tends to be of three main types. Ability-grouped class-assignment policies assign students to classes on the basis of their measured ability; thus, there is a top class, a middle class, and a bottom class. Within-class ability grouping, often used in self-contained elementary classrooms, uses flexible ability grouping: a pupil might be in the top reading group and the middle mathematics group. In regrouping plans, such as the Joplin plan used in elementary schools, students are assigned to heterogeneous classes for most of the day and are then regrouped homogeneously for reading and mathematics. In a recent review, Gutierrez and Slavin (1992) determined that such regrouping plans tend to be effective in improving student achievement.

The research on grouping by ability versus grouping heterogeneously tends to support heterogeneous grouping, although there is still some controversy about the weight of the evidence and its applications to special groups of learners, such as the gifted. After reviewing all the evidence collected over several decades, Passow (1988) concludes that "a single, inflexible approach to grouping is, therefore, inappropriate" (p. 222). He also believes the evidence indicates that grouping practices are neither unconditionally good nor bad.

The complexity and importance of the issue suggest that the faculty should carefully review the evidence for their level of schooling, assess the special needs of their students, and make decisions about grouping that seem fair, effective, flexible, and feasible.

Curriculum tracking, on the other hand, is a practice of sorting students into different curriculum tracks based on career goals. Thus, it tends to be an issue especially relevant for high schools, which usually place students into one of three tracks: general, college preparatory, or vocational. This three-track system is gradually being replaced by a two-track one: academic and vocational-technical. (For an analysis of such programs, see Bottoms, Presson, and Johnson 1992.)

There are several serious problems with the uses of rigid and sharply differentiated tracking systems (the findings below are drawn from Rosenbaum 1980; Page 1991; Hill, Foster, and Gendler 1990; and Oakes 1985). First, many students are in tracks inconsistent with their career choices. They are not sure of career plans, have much misinformation about career requirements, and often change career plans soon after graduation from high school. Also, once students are placed in a particular curriculum track, they will find it difficult to move out of it. Moving from general or vocational to college preparatory is especially difficult.

In addition, many vocational and college preparatory curriculums do not appear to provide effective preparation. Also, curriculum tracking tends to stratify the student body, creating many curricular, social, and time barriers to the interaction of students across curriculum groups. And noncollege curriculums seem to foster a delinquent subculture: students in the general and vocational tracks are more likely to report participating in such activities as drinking, smoking, playing truant, vandalizing, and gang fighting.

Another serious problem is that classes for lower-track students tend to be boring, unstimulating, routine, and devoid of challenge. Many teachers tend to resent being asked to teach lower-track students and respond by simply going through the motions of holding class. Finally, there is a serious impact on achievement. Hill, Foster, and Gendler (1990) point out that "high schools with character" offer "centripetal curricula" that draw all students to the study of core skills and knowledge. Students are not tracked into dead-end programs on the basis of premature career choices.

What should schools do in response to such negative evidence? Goodlad (1984) gives a strong and clear answer: Eliminate all curriculum tracking. Boyer (1983) offers what seems to be a more constructive solution: During the first two years of high school, provide a common "core" curriculum for all students. During the last two years, devote at least half of the time available to "elective clusters," which are carefully planned elective sequences that enable students to pursue advanced study of academic subjects or to explore career options—or both.

Although Boyer's proposals seem attractive, school leaders must deal with the reality that vocational-technical schools are deeply entrenched institutions with their own vocal constituencies. And there are enough excellent vo-tech programs to warrant their continuation, despite the fact that they are not yet supported by an extensive research base. It would therefore make more sense for high schools concerned with the issue of curriculum tracking to undertake a program of incremental improvement in dealing with the tracking problem.

Under the direction of school leaders, high school faculties could consider the following issues:

• When should students enter the vocational-technical school? Most experts now recommend that the last two years of high school provide enough time for vocational-technical education. Some even suggest that one year of full-time study during the senior year might be sufficient.

• Should the "general" curriculum track be abandoned? Many states are now recommending the elimination of such a track as being without purpose and focus. If the school is providing all students with a sound academic program in English, social studies, mathematics, and science, then counselors and teachers just have to be sure that students with any college aspirations understand the importance of studying a foreign language in high school.

• How should the school group students for instruction? Some grouping in mathematics and science probably is desirable. In English and social studies, faculties might consider offering content-option electives, letting students sort themselves out. At the least, it seems wise to encourage the social studies department to use heterogeneous grouping so that students of varied abilities and aspirations have an opportunity to exchange views about the past, present, and future. Several schools report success with such "untracking" programs (see, for example, Oakes and Lipton 1992).

• How can our school provide students with timely and useful career education? The best time for career education is probably the year before the student makes a decision about attending the vocational-technical school. You have several choices here about the delivery system for career education: for example, group guidance though the homeroom; a separate course; or a special unit in the English curriculum

• How can our school improve the career guidance offered by our counselors? Guidance counselors probably need special training in career counseling to help them avoid these common mistakes: relying too much on single test scores, being unconsciously influenced by the student's social class and ethnic background, and directing students into vocational programs rather than helping students and their parents make their own informed choices.

A careful analysis of these issues should enable a faculty to develop its own program of incremental change to ensure that its program of studies opens, not closes, doors for its students.

Criterion 6. A Sound Program of Studies Is Responsive. This criterion assesses the extent to which the program of studies is responsive to the special needs of the student population served by the school. Obviously, opinions will differ about the extent to which the curriculum should be "needs sensitive." Conservatives seem to support a curriculum confined to academic content; progressives tend to support one that deals with students' current concerns and questions that go beyond the academic content. The position advocated here is that each school should make this determination on the basis of the availability of non-school resources to address these concerns, the values of the community with respect to this issue, and the convictions and beliefs of educators.

The research on the effectiveness of curriculums dealing with current issues and needs is somewhat discouraging. In a comprehensive review of the effectiveness of "contemporary issues" curriculums, Leming (1992) determined that curriculums focusing on such issues as peace education, drug education, global education, and death education were effective in conveying knowledge but in general were not effective in changing attitudes. Leming notes, however, that curriculums emphasizing peer interaction, discussion, and exploration of attitudes in a democratic classroom environment were consistently effective in modifying attitudes.

Given the complexity and sensitivity of this issue, a careful assessment is in order. The Council should develop a survey instrument to solicit the opinions of parents, students, and teachers with respect to several specific issues. One such instrument is shown in Figure 7.5.

For best results, the survey should be administered in a setting that will give leaders an opportunity to explain their concerns, to clarify the process being used, and to assure the respondents that the returns will be a significant part of the decision-making process.

Once the results have been tallied, reduced, and systematized, the faculty can then determine how they wish to respond to needs that have a large measure of parent, teacher, and student support. Here are the options available to them:

• Add special topics to existing courses,

• Develop one comprehensive course dealing with high-priority needs, or

• Offer a series of minicourses or intensive learning experiences focusing on the issues.

FIGURE 7.5
Survey for Assessing Students' Special Needs

Tell us your opinion about whether the topics listed below should be included in our school's curriculum. Circle one of these answers: Definitely; Maybe; No.

You may also add any topics to the list that you think should definitely be included. Your responses will be analyzed and carefully considered as the faculty determine if the present curriculum is sufficiently responsive to students' needs.

1. Avoiding alcohol and drug abuse.	DEFINITELY	MAYBE	NO
2. Avoiding AIDS and other sexually transmitted diseases.	DEFINITELY	MAYBE	NO
3. Making sound moral choices.	DEFINITELY	MAYBE	NO
4. Making wise career choices.	DEFINITELY	MAYBE	NO
5. Contributing to family life.	DEFINITELY	MAYBE	NO
6. Making wise choices about sex.	DEFINITELY	MAYBE	NO
7. Becoming an intelligent consumer.	DEFINITELY	MAYBE	NO
8. Preventing suicide.	DEFINITELY	MAYBE	NO
9. Protecting the environment.	DEFINITELY	MAYBE	NO
10. Preparing for college entrance tests.	DEFINITELY	MAYBE	NO
11. Serving and improving our community.	DEFINITELY	MAYBE	NO
12. Making wise use of leisure time.	DEFINITELY	MAYBE	NO
13. Understanding the future.	DEFINITELY	MAYBE	NO
14. Developing an awareness of global issues.	DEFINITELY	MAYBE	NO
15. Reducing and dealing with group conflict.	DEFINITELY	MAYBE	NO
16. Selecting and gaining acceptance into institutions of higher education.	DEFINITELY	MAYBE	NO
17. Living in peace with other ethnic groups and nations.	DEFINITELY	MAYBE	NO
18. Coping with death and dying.	DEFINITELY	MAYBE	NO
19. Reducing racial prejudice.	DEFINITELY	MAYBE	NO
20. Preventing another Holocaust.	DEFINITELY	MAYBE	NO
21. Avoiding sex role stereotypes.	DEFINITELY	MAYBE	NO

22. Other topics you think DEFINITELY should be included:

Proposing Program Changes

Any program changes should be formalized in a specific proposal for modifying the program of studies that includes a rationale for the change and an analysis of the proposal's impact on resources. The Council should present the proposal to the faculty for final review before asking for the superintendent's review.

Restructuring the School's Program of Studies

School-based restructuring of the curriculum attempts to accomplish two key goals:

• To redefine the nature of general education by specifying what all students should know, emphasizing outcomes instead of courses and credits.

• To rethink the way learning experiences should be organized to accomplish those outcomes, focusing especially on minimizing existing subject-matter distinctions.

At the present time, the School Council will want to become familiar with five approaches to restructuring programs of study:

1. Sizer's work with his Coalition of Essential Schools focuses on a smaller range of goals in order to reduce class size and focus instruction. (See his 1992 work.)

2. Adler's Paideia Group is concerned chiefly with rethinking instructional processes. His work seems to be somewhat conservative, emphasizing the major disciplines. (See Adler 1984.)

3. Cawelti's Project on Redefining General Education seems to be bolder in its design. He reports the results of some initial attempts to redesign in Roberts and Cawelti 1984.

4. Gardner's Multiple Intelligences approach uses the following multiple intelligences as redesign concepts: linguistic, musical, logical-mathematical, spatial, bodily-kinesthetic, intrapersonal, and interpersonal (see Gardner 1991).

5. Spady's "transformational" approach to an outcome-based education curriculum (see Spady and Marshall 1991 for an explanation of this approach to restructuring).

The Council may decide to join one of the networks created to foster these approaches and to use the documents provided by that network. Or, if the Council decides to develop its own approach to restructuring, the following steps should be taken.

First, review the district guidelines to set the parameters and review the foundation documents to establish direction.

Second, determine which existing structures, other than the mastery curriculum, will be used to accomplish the school's goals. In addition to the mastery curriculum, you will probably use the activity program and the student services program. In addition, there may be special structures that should be added. Middle schools, for example, would want to include their adviser/advisee program; high schools with community service or apprenticeship programs would want to include those special opportunities.

Next, align the existing structures, including the mastery curriculum, with the school's goals. Here again, a simple matrix would be useful. Across the top are listed the existing structures; down the left side, list the educational goals of the school. For each goal, indicate with the letter *E* which existing structure will *emphasize* that goal and with the letter *R* which will reinforce that goal.

Next, set up special committees charged with ensuring that structures other than the mastery curriculum are organized to accomplish the goals allocated. Used systematically, such a process would enable adviser/advisee programs to become more goal-oriented and, one hopes, more effective.

Now turn to the mastery curriculum goals. Decide which *learning structures* you will use to accomplish the mastery goals. The learning structures are the new "courses" you will develop, although it might be better to think of them as the major concepts or themes by which learning is organized. Since this is a highly creative process, it is difficult to be formulaic about it. There are, however, some useful approaches:

• Review materials from the restructuring networks identified above to see what you can learn from them.

• Reflect on the mastery goals and try to find clusters and patterns that link them. Some schools find it useful to identify a single learning structure for each goal, although this decision may result in an overly fragmented program of studies.

• Consider existing subjects. It may well be that the best way to understand mathematical concepts and skills is through a course called "Mathematics." You should also be alert, however, to new ways in which those old courses might be linked—such as in a course called "Technological Systems" that would combine science, mathematics, and social studies.

• Consider the learners—their needs and interests.

• In thinking about new structures, you might find it useful to play with diagrams or schematics.

Here are some learning structures that might be used in a middle school program for 7th graders (the traditional subject from which their content is drawn is noted in parentheses):

• Problem Solving (math, science, social studies)
• Wellness (health, science, physical education, social studies)
• Creative Studies (language arts, technology, science, home economics, music, art)
• Community (social studies, science, language arts)
• Communication (language arts, computer science, science, social studies, art)
• Special Interests (a range of electives)

The next major step is to align the mastery goals with the learning structures, using the same general process explained in the preceding chapter.

Next, by considering the nature of the learners and the number and importance of the goals assigned to a particular learning structure, determine for each structure the approximate percentage of weekly learning time the structure will be allocated. Thinking of learning time as a percentage of total time may free planners from the limitations of the existing "period" schedule.

Now summarize your results in a large chart that shows the following: learning structures, the mastery goals each will be responsible for, and the percentage of the total program time it will require. Also, develop a sample weekly schedule showing the new learning structures, the time allocated, and how they fit into a schedule. Although you ultimately may decide to use a radical new scheduling approach (such as the intensive schedule that enables students to study only one or two subjects at a time), this is a practical test of the feasibility of your efforts.

Now have the chart and the sample schedule reviewed by interested groups: the Curriculum Planning Council, Citizens Curriculum Advisory Council, and faculty members who will be responsible for implementing the new program.

Next, develop scope-and-sequence charts for the learning structures, following the general procedures explained in Chapter 6. Finally, use the scope-and-sequence charts as the basis for writing the new units of study (this process is explained more fully in Chapter 8).

Communicating the Results

When fully developed, the renewed or restructured program of studies should be described in a special booklet given to parents, students, and teachers. Typically, the program of studies booklet should include the following elements:

• The school district's and the school's educational goals.

• The district's and the school's vision of curriculum.

• The required subjects, with brief descriptions, time allocations, and credits (where applicable).

• The elective courses available, with brief descriptions, time allocations, and credits.

• The requirements for promotion or graduation, including demonstrations or performances of competence.

• The extracurricular activities and other special learning opportunities available to students.

• Provisions for individualizing the curriculum, including special opportunities and resources for gifted and disabled students.

Determining the Need for
Additional School Curriculum Materials

Through the processes explained in this chapter, the school has identified its own educational goals and curricular vision, allocated the goals to specific programs, and renewed or restructured its program of studies. The School Council should now decide whether additional curriculum materials, aside from those explained in the next chapter, will be needed. Some types of materials that schools have developed include: an explanation of how the activity program operates and contributes to educational goals; an explanation of how the student services program operates and contributes to educational goals; a statement regarding the school's educational values and the realization of those values through the hidden curriculum and the culture and climate of the school; and a list of the organic outcomes given special emphasis and an explanation of how those outcomes are achieved. Additional materials produced at the school level should be presented to educators and parents in an integrated package, perhaps as part of the program of studies booklet.

8

Developing the Classroom Curriculum

Even in a model that values districtwide curriculum coordination and school-based program development, much important curriculum work is done at the classroom level. And whether in teams or individually, teachers perform a variety of curriculum functions.

This is not to say that teachers should develop whatever curriculum they wish. Such an approach can result in the "shopping mall" curriculum described so insightfully by Powell, Farrar, and Cohen (1985). Teachers do decide, however, the type and extent of curriculum integration. They use the district's curriculum guide to develop a syllabus for a required course. They develop a yearly schedule based on that course syllabus, showing how the mastery curriculum will be organized and delivered, and they write units of study derived from the syllabus and the yearly schedule. Finally, they also decide how the mastery curriculum will be individualized.

Integrating the Curriculum

One of the most basic decisions is whether and how the curriculum will be integrated. In the model proposed here, the decision to integrate the curriculum should be made at the school level, within the parameters of the district curriculum and the school's program of studies.

Types of Integration

There are several models of curriculum integration and several ways of classifying those models (for some alternative conceptualizations, see Jacobs 1989; Beck, Copa, and Pease 1991; Fogarty 1991; and Drake 1993). Here is a simple way of classifying these approaches while avoiding complicated jargon:

Integrating While Keeping Separate Subjects. In general, there are four ways to do this:

1. Correlate two subjects so that similar content is taught at the same time. For example, teach Colonial history and Colonial literature at the same time in different classes. Or ensure that students in mathematics class are being taught operations they need for science class.

2. Integrate skills across the disciplines (reading, writing, thinking, learning). Some experts call this *infusion.* You analyze the separate subject guides and identify ways in which these generic skills can be infused into existing subjects.

3. Integrate within the disciplines (such as whole language and unified science). Rather than teaching writing separate from reading, for instance, the teacher integrates these two aspects of language arts.

4. Integrate informally: when teaching one discipline, occasionally bring in content from another. Thus, an elementary teacher teaching social studies would have the pupils read novels about the period being studied.

Integrating Two or More Subjects. There are several ways to combine more than one subject. Here are just a few to consider:

1. Subject-focused: Use one discipline (such as history) as the organizing structure and integrate the content and skills from one or more other subjects. Thus, an American Studies course might be structured around American history but integrate content from the arts and English language arts.

2. Theme-focused: Identify a theme (such as "Families First") and use content from several disciplines.

3. Project-focused: Have students do a major project (such as studying their community) that involves several disciplines.

4. Other organizing focuses: Use focuses such as eras of history, aesthetic principles, great works, or world cultures.

Why Integrate?

There isn't much argument about the need to integrate within subjects; however, there is some debate about integrating two or more subjects. If the focus is on integration that combines or transcends the separate subjects, one of the first issues you must resolve is, "Why integrate?"

In developing a rationale to support integration, you can turn both to research and theoretical arguments. In general, research supports the use of integrated curriculums. As Vars (1991) notes, most of more than eighty normative and comparative studies have concluded that students in various types of integrated programs have performed as well as or better than students studying separate subjects.

Several theoretical arguments have also been advanced (see Shoemaker 1989 for further discussion). First, the real world is integrated, not fragmented. Typically, the problems that adults face are not compartmentalized but require the skills and knowledge of several subjects. Second, students learn best when learning is connected to what they know or are interested in. Integrated curriculums facilitate the introduction of student-related issues. Students are more motivated to study questions of importance to them—and those questions cannot be confined to a given subject. Next, integrated curriculums can save some time in the school day. If the schedule is modified appropriately, the integration of subjects can reduce time spent moving from class to class. The integrated schedule is less fragmented. Also, research on the brain tentatively suggests that the brain better retains and more readily accesses knowledge that is patterned and holistic.

Many educators, however, question the wisdom of integrating the curriculum. First, there is general agreement that critical thinking and problem solving require in-depth knowledge of the subjects (see, for example, Bransford, Vye, Kinzer, and Risko 1990). Too much integration might shortchange this important content knowledge. Second, each subject or discipline has its own way of knowing and inquiring, and these are critically important in understanding the world of knowledge (see Bruner 1960). Finally, as Brophy and Alleman (1991) note, many integrated units are poorly designed, not based upon sound principles of learning, and are thus unlikely to achieve their intended outcomes.

When deciding about integration, it would therefore seem desirable to weigh all the advantages and disadvantages and then decide, level by level, subject by subject, and model by model, how you wish to integrate. As the discussion above suggests, there is no single best type, and as

Walker and Schaffarzick (1974) note, different types of curriculums produce different patterns of achievement. In short, curriculums achieve what they are designed to achieve. If students study a focused unit on writing persuasion, they learn to write persuasively but may fail to see the connections between written persuasion and visual persuasion. If they study persuasion in several communication modes, they see the connections clearly but their persuasive writing skills may not be as well developed as they would be in a writing course.

One way to maintain the advantages of both the integrated and the subject-centered curriculum is presented below. You might consider it as simply a practical way of finding a defensible middle ground.

First, use within-subject integration to emphasize the interrelationship of concepts and skills and to make the subject more interesting to students. In doing so, however, give sufficient attention to the important skills. For example, research in general supports the desirability of a "whole language" approach that integrates the language arts; however, research also indicates that phonics and word recognition need specific attention (see, for example, Juel 1991.)

Second, give special attention to teaching reading and writing skills in science, social studies, and mathematics; those skills should not be confined to the language arts.

Next, use across-subject integration at the elementary and middle-school levels where it seems most appropriate. Elementary teachers in self-contained classrooms can integrate with the least difficulty. Most of the experts in middle-school education recommend integration as the best model for the middle-level curriculum (see, for example, Beane 1990).

In high school, give special attention to the separate disciplines. Advanced concepts in such subjects as mathematics and science are probably best learned separately (see Relan and Kimpston 1991 for a further analysis). If integration is desired, you can offer carefully designed courses that combine two subjects (such as English and social studies).

Initial Decisions About Integration

Before developing integrated units, it is important to analyze two key issues: the extent of the integration and how much existing curriculums and tests will constrain the design process. You essentially have three choices to define the extent of integration:

1. Develop integrated units to be used within an existing curriculum

and schedule. The simplest way to begin is to write units that can be used in a self-contained, multidisciplinary elementary classroom or taught by a team of middle school or high school teachers. Thus, a 4th grade team of teachers might decide to develop a unit on "Our Community," combining language arts and social studies. They each would use the unit as they desired within the existing schedule. Or a middle-school team might decide to plan and write a unit on "Change," integrating science, social studies, and language arts. They would cooperate in teaching the unit.

2. Develop an integrated course. A more ambitious approach is to plan and write a complete course that integrates two or more subjects. That course could be a quarter, a semester, or a year in length; it could be offered as an elective or as a required subject. Thus, a high school English teacher and an American history teacher might decide to plan and teach a course on "American Studies."

3. Restructure the curriculum around an integrated program. This is the most ambitious of all. You and your colleagues would decide to restructure the curriculum with a radical change in the schedule, as explained in Chapter 7.

The other important design issue is determining to what extent existing curriculums and tests will act as constraints. Most experts writing about integrated curriculums approach the subject as if there were no curriculum in place and there were no required tests. The reality is that most school districts have subject-centered curriculums in place, and the students' mastery of them is assessed through end-of-course curriculum-referenced tests.

If you don't need to worry about existing curriculums and tests, you can skip the rest of this discussion. But if you have these constraints, consider using either of the following processes (these examples assume that you are integrating 10th grade English language arts and social studies, although the processes could apply to any grade level and any subjects):

• **The yearly calendar approach.** The 10th grade English teachers develop a yearly calendar for their subject. They review the existing guides, their textbooks, and the tests and identify in chronological order the subject-matter units they plan to teach. The 10th grade social studies teachers do the same. Then they meet, review their proposed yearly schedules, and identify one or more places where the units might be integrated, with some minor modifications.

• **The curriculum analysis approach.** The two teams each review their curriculums and end-of-course tests. Based upon that review, they classify each learning objective into one of the categories: mastery, organic, and enrichment. As they design integrated units, they check to be sure that they are addressing the mastery objectives.

With these decisions made, you are ready to develop integrated units, as explained later in this chapter.

Developing a Syllabus

Some teachers find it useful to develop a course syllabus for one required subject at one grade level based on the district's mastery curriculum. Thus, a team of 4th grade teachers might collaboratively produce four course syllabuses: 4th grade reading/language arts, 4th grade mathematics, 4th grade social studies, and 4th grade science. Or they might combine them into a document entitled *Curriculum: Grade 4.*

Secondary teachers, who tend to think more in terms of courses, especially find this process useful. Elementary teachers, who seem generally to be less "course" oriented, find it less useful. The issue, therefore, should be resolved by the classroom teachers, who should exercise a high degree of autonomy with respect to the classroom curriculum.

The following process is only one of several that have been developed for producing course syllabuses. A book by Robinson, Ross, and White (1985) explains what seems to be an especially useful alternative to the following model, which assumes that teachers have been provided with a variety of tools for the subject for which they are planning: the subject goals, the scope-and-sequence chart, and the grade-level objectives from the curriculum guide.

1. Develop a Portrait of the Year. The first step is to develop a big picture that enables you to think globally before thinking particularly. Think about what you really want for the students from that year's work. Review the curriculum guide's grade-level objectives for that subject. Examine texts and other learning materials as well as end-of-course and standardized tests. Then think about the students, their needs, their interests, and their community. What are the rhythms of the year and what occurs in students' lives? Apply your own knowledge of teaching and learning and your own values with respect to that subject. In the end, summarize the results of your data-gathering and reflection. For example, this is what a team of 5th grade teachers produced as they planned a science course:

We want to make science exciting for our students, who don't always see the value of science. We want them to see science as something that touches their lives. And we want it to be a problem-solving, hands-on approach. Let's start with what they know—their rural community. We'll do some practical work in conserving the earth's resources, focusing on what they and their families can do. That also would give us a good chance to do some integrating with social studies and language arts. Since we're not too far from the ocean, we can next do some work on oceans, maybe planning an extended field trip. We have to get in a solid unit on the nature of matter and the changes in matter; maybe that could come next, since by this time they might be fired up about the importance of science. Then we could turn to another exciting topic, their bodies and the bodily systems—stressing the health aspects. We should then have them study force and machines—and then heat. By that time they should be ready for a challenging unit on the plant kingdom, again relating it to this community. We can follow up with a brief unit on fungi, algae, bacteria, and viruses—again emphasizing the health aspects.

On the other hand, a portrait developed by teachers more concerned with the logical sequence of knowledge might see the same year's work following this sequence:

- The world's most important resources
- Oceans as a key resource
- The living and nonliving elements in the oceans
- The effects of pollution on the living elements in the ocean
- The way we can reduce pollution through legislation

From this very general and somewhat subjective portrait, you can then move to a more specific and objective listing of the unit titles.

2. Identify the Titles of the Units to Be Taught. The title should indicate the main focus of the units you will teach. Several steps are involved here. First, review your "big picture." As shown in the example above, it will often refer to unit themes. Also review the curriculum guide, paying special attention to the mastery goals and curriculum objectives. Then determine the organizing principle or principles to be used in developing units. Here are some options to consider: general concepts ("Ecology"); major themes ("Families First"); complex skills ("Writing Persuasively"); time periods ("The Thirties"). Also decide how many units you will be able to teach effectively, considering the nature of the learners and the need for depth of understanding. You should also briefly review the learning materials available and the tests your students must take. The former will suggest unit titles; the latter will highlight any constraints you must take into account. Based on all these analyses, make a tentative decision about unit titles. Review them to decide if they are likely to achieve the subject goals.

3. Determine the Sequence of Units. The next step is to determine the order of the units. You might want to consider these four major sequencing principles:

- Student interests: Begin with the most interesting.
- Content difficulty: Move from easy to difficult.
- Chronology: Use a time sequence.
- Logical learning sequence: Learn Concept 1, which is necessary to understand Concept 2, and so on.

In determining unit sequence, elementary teachers should be especially sensitive to the seasonal interests of younger students and their awareness of national holidays.

4. Allocate Time to Each Unit. Time allocations are important, since time and learning are so closely related (see Walberg 1988). Time can perhaps best be represented by the number of instructional periods to be devoted to the unit. An instructional period is defined as a clearly demarcated session lasting from thirty to fifty minutes. Allocate time by following these steps:

- Calculate the total number of instructional periods available.
- Determine the relative importance and complexity of each unit.
- Allocate periods to each unit, ensuring sufficient time for depth of learning and problem solving.

5. Systematize the Decisions in the Course Syllabus. Course syllabuses take many forms. If your state or school district does not mandate a specific format, you might consider placing the syllabus in a loose-leaf binder to enable you and your colleagues to add materials and make changes easily. The syllabus should typically include the following components: the subject goals, the curriculum guide grade-level objectives, the unit titles in sequence of study, and time allocations.

With the syllabus completed, you should do one final check to be sure that all the mastery grade-level objectives are included in the units. Perhaps the easiest way to do this is to code the curriculum guide, noting for each mastery objective which unit emphasizes that outcome.

Developing Yearly Plans

Whether or not they develop course syllabuses, teachers should be required to develop and submit yearly plans, which are important for several reasons. They indicate which units will be taught, when they will be taught, and in what sequence. They also indicate the time to be allotted to each unit—a critical component in student achievement. Although ignored by many school administrators and teachers, yearly plans are a key part of the classroom curriculum.

If a course syllabus has been produced, then all the important decisions can be recorded in a yearly planning calendar. If a course syllabus is not required, then teachers can use the processes explained above to identify unit titles, sequence, and time allocations.

The calendar should list the weeks of the school year, the major events occurring throughout the year, and the title of each unit. The "major events" column is important; it serves as a reminder of school and community activities that may interfere with teaching and learning. The column would note such events as national and state holidays, vacations, parent meetings, and major social events (such as the Senior Prom). You may also decide to include other information on the calendar, such as the type of unit, the mastery objectives taught in the unit, the resources needed, and the total number of periods allocated to the unit. Whatever information teachers consider important to yearly planning should be included.

The format of the calendar is not important. An example of the format suggested above, which works well for one subject, is shown in Figure 8.1. Many elementary teachers use a different format with the subjects listed down the left side of the chart and the weeks of the school year across the top. They enter in the appropriate column the titles of the units they plan to teach.

For further analysis of how principals can support yearly planning, see Glatthorn 1993b.

Writing Units of Study

Units written by teachers are one of the most important components of the classroom curriculum. Unit planning is much more significant in the learning process than daily planning because the unit level is best for using integration and for showing problem solving at work. Following is one process for developing units based upon a constructivist

FIGURE 8.1
Sample Yearly Plan

Dates	Major Events	Unit Title	Unit Title	Key Mastery Objectives	Resources
Sept. 4–8	Yom Kippur	Keeping a journal	Focused	Use journal as a record of major events	Amiel's journal
Sept. 11–15		Semiotics: Reading the Sights	Integrated English	Interpret signs of the local culture	*The Signs of Our Times* (Solomon)
Sept. 18–22	Parents Night	See above			

approach to teaching and learning. Constructivism emphasizes the learner as a maker of meaning and a solver of problems. (For a useful discussion of constructivism, see Brooks and Brooks 1993.) Rather than teaching thinking skills in isolation, teachers using a constructivist approach emphasize active thinking and processing of information throughout the unit, generally following a process that includes these steps:

1. Consider Integration. The first step is to decide on the extent of curriculum integration you wish to achieve, as explained earlier.

2. Block in the Unit. The blocking process establishes the general parameters within which you will work. You make several decisions—or confirm some decisions previously made:

• The title of the unit, which should make clear the general emphasis of the unit—for example, "Our Changing Language."

• The length of the unit, if you have not previously decided this. Keep in mind the importance of curriculum depth as well as students' developmental stage and attention span. A general rule of thumb is "The older the student, the longer the unit." For our sample unit on language, we'll tentatively allocate two weeks.

• The unit goals or outcomes, which are general statements of what you want students to learn. A shorter unit will probably have one objective; longer units may have as many as four. Unlike the more specific lesson objectives, the unit outcomes will often be stated generally. Consider using language that clearly implies a critical-thinking or problem-solving orientation. Here are some examples: think critically about television, solve a problem relating to language change, use concepts of semiotics to interpret the culture critically, understand the ecology of the tundra, understand climate change and predict changes, or understand how families are changing and predict further changes.

3. Identify the Problem to Be Solved. You or the students should identify a problem or a set of problems to be solved in the unit. A problem can be construed in several ways, but the following analysis draws from and modifies the typology suggested by Marzano (1992).

- Decision making, which answers the question "What should we do?" or "What should have been done?"
- Investigation, which answers the question "What happened?"
- Experimental inquiry, which answers the question "How can this phenomenon be explained?"
- Problem solving, which answers the question "How can we achieve this goal?"
- Invention, which answers the question "What new product or approach can we develop?"

Problems can often be derived from the grade-level objectives. You can also think of questions that can lead to problems; the heuristics shown in Figure 8.2 may help you with this approach. You can use these heuristics in a variety of ways. First, you can apply them to a set of themes or concepts, such as the following: family, friends, culture, conflict, regions and places, ethnic groups and genders, eras and ages, environments, careers. Thus, using Heuristic 5 in Figure 8.2 (What different perspectives do people have about it?) in connection with the theme "Careers" might yield this problem:

> How do the following people view the role of the principal: the principal, teachers, students, parents, the superintendent, or the school board?

You can use these same heuristics to examine the several components of the subject or subjects you are focusing on. For example, you can apply Heuristic 13 to the study of communication to identify this problem: How are electronic media (such as the computer) affecting the way we communicate?

You can also focus on the students by having them generate questions they would like to answer. In facilitating this process, you may wish to teach them a simplified version of these same heuristics. After students

FIGURE 8.2
Heuristic for Identifying Problems

What is its nature?
1. What is it?
2. What does it mean?
3. What is its structure? How can we make a model of it? What are its parts?
4. How would you classify it?
5. What different perspectives do people have about it?
6. How does it operate?
7. What patterns can be seen in its various manifestations?
8. What is wrong with it and how would you fix it?

What are its relationships?
9. How is it similar to and different from others in its class?
10. What is its quality in comparison with others?
11. What inferences and generalizations can be drawn from it?
12. What are its causes and its effects?
13. How and why is it changing?
14. What were its past forms, what are its present forms, and what will be its future forms?

What are the options with respect to it?
15. What are your values with respect to it?
16. How can it be improved?
17. What are your choices with respect to it?
16. What new forms or uses of it can we create?

list several specific questions they would like to answer, you can then assist them in grouping the individual questions into one or two general problem statements.

Another way to identify problems is to begin with the materials available. Problem-solving units work best when students can gain access to and use a body of knowledge. If you have a good collection of materials on a topic such as advertising, you can review them to see what problems they suggest.

After tentatively identifying the problem to be solved, think about the unit outcome you had previously stated. Consider several factors: the time available, the students' knowledge and interests, and the materials available. This reflection may suggest the need to reframe the unit outcome—to modify its general thrust or to more sharply focus the outcome. In the example used here, the problem of language change seems too broad and demanding for 8th grade students, especially since only two weeks have been allocated to the unit. Thus, the unit outcome might be restated in these words: "Explain how and why the vocabulary of a language changes."

4. Draft the Unit Scenario. The next step is not ordinarily found in curriculum texts, but it is has been found to be especially effective in working with classroom teachers. The *unit scenario* is a script for the unit, similar to the portrait of the year. It explains in general form how the unit begins, how it moves through the stages of learning, and how it ends. It includes some reference to the major ways the students will learn. In brief, before you get into the details of the lesson objectives and activities, you describe the big picture.

You develop the scenario by first reflecting, imagining, and brainstorming in a somewhat freewheeling manner. As ideas crystallize, you jot them down. You continue until you have a clear mental picture of the major components and flow of the unit. The final step is to write a clear draft that can guide you and your colleagues. Here is the first draft of the unit scenario for the unit on vocabulary change:

> Start by having students interview grandparents on words used today that were not used when they were in high school, such as *laser.* Have them use the results to make some preliminary generalizations. Maybe then set up expert groups, each one studying in depth one way that words come into the language. After studying how, then move into why—technology, societal changes, immigration patterns. Close with predicting some new words for the year 2000.

When you have finished the first draft of the scenario, check it against the criteria for unit excellence identified in Step 8 on page 104. This is only a preliminary check, to ensure that you are moving in the right direction.

5. Determine Knowledge Needed and Means of Access. With the scenario in mind, think about the knowledge needed and how students will gain access to it. Students can best solve problems when they have in-depth knowledge relative to the problem. This unit model synthesizes content and process, rather than approaching them as separate entities, so students acquire knowledge and then use that knowledge in solving the problem.

Knowledge is defined here as information—facts, terms, dates, names, or generalizations. *Generative knowledge* is knowledge that is used in solving problems. To identify the knowledge needed, you think about the scenario and then focus on the problem, asking yourself this question: "If I were solving the problem, what knowledge would I need?" You then adapt your knowledge needs to the students' developmental level. To solve the problem of vocabulary change, students will need to know the types of vocabulary change and the factors affecting vocabulary change.

You also should think about the most efficient and effective means for students to get access to that knowledge. In making this decision, consider the students' age, the nature of the knowledge, and the materials readily available—or those that you are willing to produce. Here are several ways that students can access knowledge:

- Listening to the teacher present information
- Guided discovery
- Guided discussion
- Interviewing experts, parents, and others
- Learning from peers
- Reading texts and other print materials
- Using computer software
- Viewing television
- Using other media

These resources for knowledge acquisition provide the raw materials for problem solving; they embody the generative knowledge that students will need to solve the problem. All problem-solving units will require students to gain access to and use such knowledge resources. In our sample unit, the following resources might prove useful:

- Collections of new words that have recently come into the language
- Short stories from several periods of history illustrating vocabulary change
- Articles bemoaning and welcoming vocabulary change
- Teacher-written materials on vocabulary change

6. Determine Which Learning Strategies Students Will Need to Learn. Learning strategies are the mental operations that help in the problem-solving process. Some are generic, such as using web diagrams to suggest connections; some are subject-specific, such as listing all the known elements in solving mathematical problems. These strategies are better taught in context, not in isolation.

7. Sketch the Lesson Plans. With the unit-level planning completed, move to the lesson level. But you don't develop lessons *de novo*; you develop them from all the work you've done thus far at the unit planning level. Thus, a lesson is derived from the unit and a unit is not a random collection of lessons. Several lesson-planning models are available. If teachers have a good unit structure to build from, however, they ordinarily don't need special instruction in planning lessons.

8. Evaluate and Disseminate the Unit. The unit should be carefully evaluated before it is disseminated. To guide the process of unit evaluation, apply the following criteria:

• The unit is focused on outcomes: the unit goal or key outcome is clearly stated, and the lesson objectives or outcomes are directly related to the unit goal.

• The unit appropriately integrates content from the subject (or from two or more subjects) and uses writing and reading as ways of learning.

• The unit emphasizes depth, not superficiality, with sufficient time provided to achieve depth of understanding.

• The unit focuses on problem solving and critical thinking in the context of real situations.

• The unit has appropriate sequence and coherence so that lessons build on and relate to each other.

• The unit fosters a constructivist approach to learning.

• The unit emphasizes a social context for learning, with effective use of cooperative learning and student interaction.

• The learning activities recommended are directly related to the outcomes, are likely to achieve the outcomes, and are developmentally appropriate.

• The unit makes appropriate provisions for individual differences and is especially sensitive to the needs and strengths of students from minority ethnic groups.

• The unit provides for authentic assessment of student learning.

The final step is to prepare the unit for peer review and dissemination. You systematize all the previous decisions, add the necessary details, and prepare a review draft for colleagues to evaluate the unit. If your school district does not require you to use a standard format, you might consider using this format: Start with a cover page that identifies the title of the unit, the school district, the school and its address, the authors' names, and the year of publication. The next page is a table of contents. The third page provides an overview of the unit with the following information: title, recommended grade level, type of unit, suggested time allocation, unit outcomes, required resources, and the means by which students will demonstrate learning. That third page is followed by the individual lessons. The last sections of the unit are a comprehensive list of additional resources and a unit evaluation form.

Individualizing the Curriculum

Decisions about individualizing the curriculum should also be made at the classroom level. The term *individualize* is used here in the sense of making explicit provisions for adapting the curriculum to students' particular abilities and needs. In this sense, the concept is broad and goes far beyond the narrow view of providing for self-pacing. Several components of the curriculum and the instructional processes can be individualized:

- Content emphases
- Skills to be mastered
- Level of achievement expected
- Pace of learning
- Method of learning
- Learning environment provided
- Degree of learning structure
- Learning materials
- Type and amount of feedback
- Means of final assessment
- Personal meaning

The following discussion explains some processes that you and your colleagues can use in individualizing the curriculum.

Review the Models of Individualization

You should begin by reviewing the several models available for individualizing curriculums. Some of them focus on one of the aspects noted above; a few attempt to combine several.

1. *Studio or workshop model:* The teacher explains, demonstrates, and identifies outcomes expected. Each student works on a project. The instructor gives individualized feedback and further explanations and demonstrations as needed.

2. *Content option model:* The teacher identifies core skills to be mastered and designs content-option electives that include all the core skills. Students choose content-option electives.

3. *Learning centers model:* The teacher designs a learning environment that includes several learning centers, each of which uses a different medium and modality or focuses on a special aspect of the curriculum. Students rotate through learning centers according to their needs and preferences.

4. *Self-instructional model:* The teacher assesses entering competencies and places each student appropriately in a sequence of learning experiences. Students use self-instructional materials to pace their own learning. Many self-instructional models use computer-assisted instruction.

5. *Mastery learning model:* The teacher gives group instruction, assesses learning, and provides for individual remediation and enrichment.

6. *Cooperative learning model:* Students work in cooperative learning groups, with each student contributing to and learning from the group task.

7. *Peer tutoring model:* Students who need extra help are assigned an individual tutor for additional remediation and assistance.

8. *Team learning and individualized instruction:* Students work first in teams to acquire basic mastery. They then work individually for remediation or enrichment.

9. *Learning styles accommodations:* The teacher assesses students' learning styles and modality preferences and makes special accommodations to strengths and preferences.

Assess the Effectiveness of the Models

The next step is to review the research on these models, which strongly supports at least three of them: cooperative learning (Slavin 1990); peer tutoring (Levin, Glass, and Meister 1984); and team learning and individualized instruction (Slavin 1990). The research is generally negative about the effectiveness of self-paced instruction, an intervention much advocated two decades ago that seems to have resurfaced with the current interest in outcome-based education. Essentially, this approach to individualization uses a diagnostic-prescription model in which the teacher diagnoses students' needs, prescribes certain activities, and monitors students as they progress independently in a self-paced mode. While the model seems attractive, its drawbacks are obvious. Such approaches typically place too much emphasis on learning in isolation. Current theory and research stress the importance of social and cooperative learning. Also, students often report that the materials are boring. And students are not given sufficient direction by the teacher. (See Slavin 1984 for a critique.) Most reviews of research conclude that these individualized programs are no more effective than traditional instruction (Bangert, Kulik, and Kulik 1983).

The research seems inconclusive with respect to mastery learning. As initially formulated by Benjamin Bloom and adapted by Block and Anderson (1975), mastery learning was widely touted in the 1970s. It has reappeared as a recommended strategy in much of the literature on outcome-based education (Spady 1988). Its significant features are these: clearly specified objectives; brief assessment measures; preset mastery performance standards; brief, focused learning units; frequent feedback to students on progress, and remediation for those requiring it.

Early research was somewhat positive about the effects of the mastery learning approach (see Guskey and Gates 1985). However, a later and more critical analysis of the research led Slavin (1987, p. 45) to conclude that the effects of mastery learning as measured by experimenter-made tests were "moderate at best" and "essentially nil on standardized achievement measures." Other critics noted that any advantages accruing from the use of mastery learning more likely came from the additional time provided than from any special feature of the mastery approach (see Good and Brophy 1991). Since the research is somewhat inconclusive, schools should carefully evaluate their own approach to mastery learning before instituting it on a widespread scale.

Research is similarly inconclusive with respect to learning styles. It confirms that learners process information in different ways and have different preferences as to how they learn. But these obvious differences have led learning styles advocates to recommend that teachers provide varied methods in varied environments to accommodate students' needs (see, for example, Dunn and Griggs 1988.) These advocates buttress their claims by citing several studies indicating that such provisions lead to improved achievement.

There are, however, several problems with the rationale, the empirical evidence, and the classroom feasibility of this accommodation approach. Several experts have rejected the rationale that teachers should accommodate individual preferences; they respond that learners need to learn in a variety of ways anyway. Critics have also noted that almost all the research supporting the use of learning styles has been completed by doctoral students serving under the direction of professors with a vested interest in learning styles. Finally, practitioners question whether classroom teachers with large classes can practically provide for several different environments and methods for students to learn. (For a critique of the research supporting the use of learning styles, see Curry 1990.)

One program that seems to hold promise, *4MAT*, provides all students with learning experiences that systematically vary the type of activity and mental processing involved. One study concluded that use of the *4MAT* program led to higher achievement of objective knowledge and better attitudes toward learning than did a "textbook" approach; however, a performance test that measured synthesis and evaluation showed no significant differences between classes using *4MAT* and those using a more traditional approach (Wilkerson and White 1988).

Based on your analysis of such research and your assessment of your own and your colleagues' knowledge of students and the community, you will eventually select a model to use. Become fully informed about it through reading, visitations, and discussions, and seek out any staff development you might need.

9

Conducting a Curriculum Audit to Ensure Quality

With all of the foregoing tasks completed, you may wish to conduct a curriculum audit to ensure quality. Curriculum auditing is a process of evaluating the management policies and procedures used to support the curriculum. Obviously, an audit can be conducted at any time the district finds convenient, but the timing recommended here is after the district has accomplished the major tasks of curriculum development. Thus, the audit becomes a quality control mechanism, not a diagnosis of needs.

Fenwick English, who is the chief advocate and primary expert in the field, has developed a comprehensive auditing process that is widely used by audit teams trained and sponsored by AASA, the American Association of School Administrators (see English 1992). This chapter proposes an audit model for those who find the AASA model too comprehensive in its approach or too demanding of resources. The following audit model is more focused and emphasizes the bottom line: student achievement.

Selecting the Audit Team

The first step is to select those who will perform the audit, or the audit team. Three types of groups may be used: an in-house team, composed solely of district representatives; an external team, composed solely of external experts; or a collaborative team, composed of both district and external representatives.

English recommends that an external team conduct the audit to ensure objectivity. The specific make-up of such an external team will depend, of course, on the scope of the audit and the resources available. To assure the cooperation and involvement of state and regional educators and to improve the quality of the audit, a representative of the state or the regional office should be included and should also review the audit design. Obviously, a district that lacks the resources needed to retain external representatives may audit itself with the understanding that a certain objectivity has been lost.

I believe that a collaborative process involving both internal and external auditors is more cost efficient and productive, although there has been no systematic study of this issue. A typical audit team of this type encompasses the following roles:

• *Audit Chair:* Manages and coordinates the audit; writes the proposal and the report; assists with other tasks as needed.

• *Audit Co-Chair:* Assists with management and coordination; completes tasks as assigned.

• *Quantitative Analysis Consultant:* Analyzes test results and survey data; performs other quantitative analyses.

• *Auditors:* Complete tasks as assigned.

Identifying the Audit Criteria

The first major task of the audit team is to identify the criteria that will be used in the auditing process. While English uses a standard set of criteria in all AASA audits, a negotiated audit agenda is recommended here.

The recommended criteria shown in Figure 9.1 have been derived by reviewing the research on student achievement and the current literature on each component, emphasizing those elements that have a direct relationship to curriculum. Thus, two types of elements are not included:

• Curriculum-related components not directly associated with improved student learning (such as the existence of a curriculum philosophy), and

• Factors associated with improved learning that are not directly related to curriculum (such as the nature of school and classroom climate).

FIGURE 9.1
Conceptual Framework: The Bottom-Line Audit Model

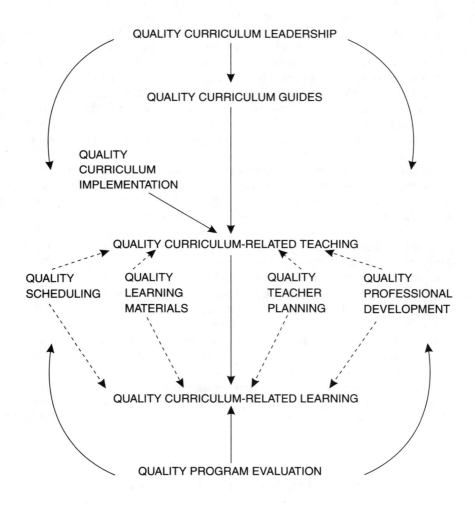

The conceptual structure of the criteria can best be understood by analyzing the framework in Figure 9.1. This bottom-line model emphasizes the learned curriculum—what students actually are learning. As Figure 9.1 shows, *quality curriculum-related learning* is the central issue. *Quality curriculum-related teaching* is the factor that most directly affects the learned curriculum. *Quality curriculum-related teaching* relies chiefly upon *quality curriculum guides,* but *quality curriculum implementation* is essential for these guides to have an impact. (Review Chapter 6 for a discussion of the implementation process.)

Four elements support quality teaching and also affect quality learning. The first element is *quality scheduling,* which is used here as a general concept that subsumes issues of time allocation, grouping practices, and staffing. While some curriculum theorists ignore the schedule as a purely "technical" issue, it is the chief instrument by which scarce resources are allocated and by which crucial tracking and grouping decisions are operationalized.

Second, *quality learning materials* in the form of textbooks, computer software, and other media are required to support quality teaching and influence quality learning. Next, *quality teacher planning* is necessary to guide the teacher and optimize student learning. Finally, *quality professional development* (including quality staff development and supervision) is needed to support quality teaching. While professional development does not have a direct impact upon student learning, effective programs do have a discernible indirect effect upon it.

Two contextual elements influence all of the previous elements. First, there should be *quality program evaluation*—that is, systematic formative and summative evaluation of all the central and supportive elements to ensure that they are in fact achieving a high level of quality. Finally, there is a need for *quality curriculum leadership* that pulls all these elements together.

Observe that there is no direct examination of the budget. It is assumed that all the quality elements require sufficient fiscal resources. Thus, aspects of budget will be examined in the context of these other issues.

Selecting Specific Audit Issues

The specific audit issues for each of the quality components are detailed in the Appendix on page 121. They have been derived from a review of the research and the current literature, and the primary source for each criterion is noted at the end of each section.

The audit team should review all the criteria presented in the Appendix, add any they think necessary, and prioritize the total set of criteria. One useful way to prioritize criteria is for audit team members to individually rank each criterion: 3, high priority; 2, medium priority; 1, low priority. With the ratings totaled, the audit team reviews the entire list and, on the basis of both need and resources, determines which criteria will be assessed. Their decisions are presented to the superintendent for review.

Developing and Implementing the Audit Design

With the criteria identified, the team should then develop and implement the audit design. The process generally includes these key steps:

1. Develop the design. The audit design specifies the criteria to be examined, indicates the methods to be used, and designates the data source for each criterion and method. The methods include interviews, observations, surveys, or document analyses. Possible data sources include the school board, district and school administrators and supervisors, teachers, other professional staff, students, parents, and documents. The scope and depth of the design will obviously depend on the resources available: time, funds, and people.

2. Develop or acquire data-collection instruments. The next step is to develop the instruments needed to conduct the audit. Data-collection instruments can include interview protocols, observation guides, surveys, and document analysis guidelines.

3. Determine who will implement the design. The next step is to identify those responsible for implementing each component of the audit design. Again, a collaborative process is recommended, with the audit team assigning certain components to district educators and other components to external representatives. For example, the district's Director of Testing might be given the task of analyzing all student test results.

4. Develop a formal audit proposal. The above decisions should be formalized and systematized in an audit proposal submitted to the school board for approval. The proposal should include the following:

- A rationale for the audit
- The audit design, methods, and instruments
- Those responsible for implementing the design

- The nature of the final report
- A time line for all key events
- A budget

5. Orient the community and staff. The staff should first be informed and oriented by the principal at the school level, using a handout developed to assist in this process. Then the community should be informed, with press releases and newsletters describing the nature and purposes of the audit. Special meetings should be held for parent-teacher organizations.

6. Conduct the audit. The audit team then carries out the audit design, according to the established schedule. Auditors should inform the audit chair of any problems that emerge during the audit.

7. Prepare the audit report. The audit report should include an executive summary, the audit design, audit results organized by criteria, and recommendations for actions to be taken. Ordinarily, the team should produce a first draft to be reviewed by the district leadership team, giving them an opportunity to clarify any misunderstandings or interpretations or to suggest alternative language that might be less controversial; however, the district leaders should not make any substantive changes that cannot be accepted by the audit team.

In the end, the results of the audit should be used to develop an action plan for improving quality learning. The data could be included in the district's strategic plan or used in a separate curriculum improvement project.

References

Adler, M. J. (1984). *The Paideia Program: An Educational Syllabus.* New York: Macmillan.

Aguayo, R. (1990). *Dr. Deming.* New York: Simon & Schuster.

Alexander, K. L., and A. M. Pallas. (1983). *Curriculum Reform and School Performance: An Evaluation of the "New Basics."* Baltimore, Md.: Center for the Social Organization of Schools, Johns Hopkins University.

Bailey, W. J. (1991). *School-Site Management Applied.* Lancaster, Pa.: Technomic.

Bangert, R. L., J. A. Kulik, and C. C. Kulik. (Summer 1983). "Individualized Systems of Instruction in Secondary Schools." *Review of Educational Research* 53, 2: 143–158.

Beane, J. A. (1990). *A Middle School Curriculum: From Rhetoric to Reality.* Columbus, Ohio: National Middle School Association.

Beck, R. H., G. H. Copa, and V. H. Pease. (October 1991). "Vocational and Academic Teachers Work Together." *Educational Leadership* 49, 2: 29–32.

Berlin, B. M., J. A. Kavanagh, and K. Jensen. (September 1988). "The Principal as Curriculum Leader: Expectations vs. Performance." *NASSP Bulletin* 72, 509: 43–49.

Bird, T. (1986). "Mutual Adaptation and Mutual Accomplishment: Images of Change in a Field Experiment." In *Rethinking School Improvement: Research, Craft, and Concept,* edited by A. Lieberman. New York: Teachers College Press.

Block, J., and L. Anderson. (1975). *Mastery Learning in Classroom Instruction.* New York: Macmillan.

Bonstingl, J. J. (1992). *Schools of Quality: An Introduction to Total Quality Management in Education.* Alexandria, Va.: ASCD.

Bottoms, G., A. Presson, and M. Johnson. (1992). *Making High Schools Work Through Integration of Academic and Vocational Education.* Atlanta, Ga.: Southern Regional Education Board.

Boyer, E. L. (1983). *High School: A Report on Secondary Education in America.* New York: Harper & Row.

Brandt, R. S., and R. W. Tyler. (1983). "Goals and Objectives." In *Fundamental Curriculum Decisions*, edited by F. W. English. Alexandria, Va.: ASCD.

Bransford, J. D., N. Vye, C. Kinzer, and V. Risko. (1990). "Teaching Thinking and Content Knowledge: Toward an Integrated Approach." In *Dimensions of Thinking and Cognitive Instruction*, edited by B. F. Jones and L. Idol. Hillsdale, N.J.: Lawrence Erlbaum.

Brookover, W. B. (1980). *Measuring and Attaining the Goals of Education.* Alexandria, Va.: ASCD.

Brooks, J. G., and M. G. Brooks. (1993). *In Search of Understanding: The Case for Constructivist Classrooms.* Alexandria, Va.: ASCD.

Brophy, J., and J. Alleman. (October 1991). "A Caveat: Curriculum Integration Isn't Always a Good Idea." *Educational Leadership* 49, 2: 66.

Bruner, J. S. (1960). *The Process of Education.* Cambridge, Mass.: Harvard University Press.

Capper, C. A., and M. T. Jamison. (1993). "Let the Buyer Beware: Total Quality Management and Educational Research and Practice." *Educational Researcher* 22, 8: 15–30.

Consortium for Policy Research in Education. (1993). "Developing Content Standards: Creating a Process for Change." *CPRE Policy Briefs* 10: 1–7.

Cooperman, P. (1978). *The Literacy Hoax.* New York: Morrow.

Cotton, K. (1990). *Effective Schooling Practices: A Research Synthesis, 1990 Update.* Portland, Ore.: Northwest Regional Educational Laboratory.

Curry, B., and T. Temple. (1992). *Using Curriculum Frameworks for Systemic Reform.* Alexandria, Va.: ASCD.

Curry, L. (October 1990). "A Critique of the Research on Learning Styles." *Educational Leadership* 48, 2: 50–56.

Deming, W. E. (1986). *Out of the Crisis.* Cambridge: Massachusetts Institute of Technology.

Drake, S. (1993). *Planning Integrated Curriculum: The Call to Adventure.* Alexandria, Va.: ASCD.

Dunn, R., and S. A. Griggs. (1988). *Learning Styles: Quiet Revolution in American Secondary Schools.* Reston, Va.: National Association of Secondary School Principals.

Elmore, R., and G. Sykes. (1992). "Curriculum Policy." In *Handbook of Research on Curriculum*, edited by P. W. Jackson. New York: Macmillan.

English, F. W. (1992). *Deciding What to Teach and Test: Developing, Aligning, and Auditing the Curriculum.* Newbury Park, Calif.: Corwin.

Educational Research Service. (Winter 1992). "Goals of the Education Curriculum: Opinions of Teachers and Principals." *ERS Spectrum.* 10, 1: 40–45.

Fielding, G. (1990). *Curriculum Leaders' Handbook.* Albany, Ore.: Linn-Benton Education Service District.

Fogarty, R. (October 1991). "Ten Ways to Integrate Curriculum." *Educational Leadership* 49, 2: 61–65.

Fuchs, L. S., D. Fuchs, C. L. Hamlett, and P. M. Stecker. (Fall 1991). "Effects of Curriculum-Based Measurement and Consultation on Teacher Planning and

Student Achievement in Mathematics Operations." *American Educational Research Journal* 28, 3: 617–641.

Fullan, M. (1991). *The New Meaning of Educational Change.* New York: Teachers College Press.

Fullan, M. (1993). "Innovation, Reform, and Restructuring Strategies." In *Challenges and Achievements of American Education*, edited by G. Cawelti. Alexandria, Va.: ASCD.

Gardner, H. (1991). *The Unschooled Mind: How Schools Should Teach.* New York: Basic Books.

Glasser, W. (1992). *The Quality School: Managing Students Without Coercion.* 2nd ed. New York: Harper Collins.

Glatthorn, A. A. (1986a). "Curriculum Reform and At-Risk Youth." In *Rethinking Reform: The Principal's Dilemma*, edited by H. J. Walberg and J. W. Keefe. Reston, Va.: National Association of Secondary School Principals.

Glatthorn, A. A. (1986b). "How Does the School Schedule Affect Curriculum?" In *Rethinking Reform: The Principal's Dilemma*, edited by H. J. Walberg and J. W. Keefe. Reston, Va.: National Association of Secondary School Principals.

Glatthorn, A. A. (1990). *Supervisory Leadership.* New York: Harper Collins.

Glatthorn, A. A. (1993a). *Criteria for Evaluating Curriculum Guides.* Greenville, N.C.: School of Education, East Carolina University.

Glatthorn, A. A. (1993b). "Teacher Planning: A Foundation for Effective Instruction." *NASSP Bulletin* 77, 551: 1–7.

Glatthorn, A. A., and N. Spencer. (1986). *Middle School/Junior High Principal's Handbook.* Englewood Cliffs, N.J.: Prentice Hall.

Good, T. L., and J. E. Brophy. (1991). *Looking in Classrooms.* 5th ed. New York: Harper and Row.

Goodlad, J. I. (1984). *A Place Called School.* New York: McGraw Hill.

Goodlad, J. I., and J. Oakes. (February 1988). "We Must Offer Equal Access to Knowledge." *Educational Leadership* 45, 6: 16–22.

Griffin, G. A. (1988). "Leadership for Curriculum Improvement: The School Administrator's Role." In *Critical Issues in Curriculum*, edited by L.N. Tanner. Chicago: University of Chicago Press.

Guskey, T. R., and S. L. Gates. (April 1985). *A Synthesis of Research on Group-Based Mastery Learning Programs.* Paper presented at meeting of American Educational Research Association, Chicago.

Gutierrez, R., and R. E. Slavin. (1992). "Achievement Effects of the Nongraded School: A Best Evidence Synthesis." *Review of Educational Research* 62: 333–376.

Herman, J. L., L. L. Morris, and C. T. Fitz-Gibbon. (1987). *Evaluator's Handbook.* Newbury Park, Calif.: Sage

Hill, P. T., G. E. Foster, and T. Gendler. (1990). *High Schools with Character.* Santa Monica, Calif.: Rand.

Hodgkinson, H. (1992). *A Demographic Look at Tomorrow.* Washington, D.C.: Institute for Educational Leadership and Center for Demographic Policy.

Huberman, A. M., and M. B. Miles. (1986). "Rethinking the Quest for School Improvement: Some Findings From the DESSI Study." In *Rethinking School Improvement: Research, Craft, and Concept*, edited by A. Lieberman. New York: Teachers College Press.

Jacobs, H. H. (1989). "Design Options for an Integrated Curriculum." In *Interdisciplinary Curriculum: Design and Implementation*, edited by H. H. Jacobs. Alexandria, Va.: ASCD.

Juel, C. (1991). "Beginning Reading." In *Handbook of Reading Research: Vol. II*, edited by R. Barr, M. L. Kamil, P. B Mosenthal, and P. D. Pearson. New York: Longman.

Lee, V. E., A. S. Bryk, and J. B. Smith. (1993). "The Organization of Effective Secondary Schools." In *Review of Research in Education 19*, edited by L. Darling-Hammond. Washington, D.C.: American Educational Research Association.

Leming, J. S. (1992). "The Influence of Contemporary Issues Curricula on School-Aged Youth." In *Review of Research in Education 18*, edited by G. Grant. Washington, D.C.: American Educational Research Association.

Levin, H. M., G. V. Glass, and G. R. Meister. (1984). *Cost Effectiveness of Four Educational Interventions*. Stanford, Calif.: Institute for Research on Educational Finance and Governance.

Loucks-Horsley, S., and S. Stiegelbauer. (1991). "Using Knowledge of Change to Guide Staff Development." In *Staff Development for Education in the '90s*, edited by A. Lieberman and L. Miller. 2nd ed. New York: Teachers College Press.

Marsh, D. D., and A. R. Odden. (1991). "Implementation of the California Mathematics and Science Curriculum Frameworks." In *Education Policy Implementation*, edited by A. R. Odden. Albany, N.Y.: SUNY Press.

Marzano, R. J. (1992). *A Different Kind of Classroom: Teaching with Dimensions of Learning*. Alexandria, Va.: ASCD.

Moore, C. M. (1987). *Group Techniques for Idea Building*. Newbury Park, Calif.: Sage.

Mora, C., and C. P. Kearney. (April 1991). *Curriculum Composition: The Reform Movement and Student Outcomes*. Paper presented at meeting of American Educational Research Association, Chicago.

Murphy, J. (1990). "Instructional Leadership: Focus on Curriculum Responsibilities." *NASSP Bulletin 74*, 525: 1–4.

Murphy, J. (1991). *Restructuring Schools: Capturing and Assessing the Phenomena*. New York: Teachers College Press.

Muther, C. (program consultant). (1985). *The Pitfalls of Textbook Adoption and How to Avoid Them* (videotape and user's manual). Alexandria, Va.: ASCD.

Oakes, J. (1985). *Keeping Track: How Schools Structure Inequality*. New Haven, Conn.: Yale University Press.

Oakes, J., and M. Lipton. (1992). "Detracking Schools: Early Lessons From the Field." *Phi Delta Kappan 73*: 448–454.

Page, R. N. (1991). *Lower-Track Classrooms: A Curricular and Cultural Perspec-*

tive. New York: Teachers College Press.

Passow, A. H. (1988). "Issues of Access to Knowledge: Grouping and Tracking." In *Critical Issues in Curriculum*, edited by L.N. Tanner. Chicago: University of Chicago Press.

Powell, A. G., E. Farrar, and D. K. Cohen. (1985). *The Shopping Mall High School.* Boston: Houghton Mifflin.

Prawat, R. S. (1993). "The Role of the Principal in the Development of Learning Communities." *Wingspread* 9: 7–9.

Relan, A., and R. Kimpston. (April 1991). *Curriculum Integration: A Critical Analysis of Practical and Conceptual Issues.* Paper presented at meeting of American Educational Research Association, Chicago.

Roberts, A. D., and G. Cawelti. (1984). *Redefining General Education in the American High School.* Alexandria, Va.: ASCD.

Robinson, F. G., J. A. Ross, and F. White. (1985). *Curriculum Development for Effective Instruction.* Toronto: Ontario Institute for Studies in Education.

Rosenbaum, J. E. (1980). "Social Implications of Educational Grouping." In *Review of Research in Education 8*, edited by D.C. Berliner. Washington, D.C.: American Educational Research Association.

Shoemaker, B. J. (1989). *Integrative Education: A Curriculum for the Twenty-First Century.* Eugene: Oregon School Study Council.

Sizer, T. R. (1985). *Horace's Compromise: The Dilemma of the American High School.* Boston: Houghton Mifflin.

Sizer, T. R. (1992). *Horace's School: Redesigning the American High School.* Boston: Houghton Mifflin.

Slavin, R. E. (January 1984). "Component Building: A Strategy for Research-Based Instruction." *Elementary School Journal* 84, 3: 255–269.

Slavin, R. E. (1987). *Mastery Learning Reconsidered.* Baltimore, Md.: Center for Research on Elementary and Middle Schools, Johns Hopkins University.

Slavin, R. E. (1990). *Cooperative Learning: Theory, Research, and Practice.* Englewood Cliffs, N.J.: Prentice Hall.

Smith, W. A., and D. J. Hindi. (1992). *Project Report: Total Quality Education in North Carolina.* Raleigh: North Carolina Quality Leadership Foundation.

Snyder, J., F. Bolin, and K. Zumwalt. (1992). "Curriculum Implementation." In *Handbook of Research on Curriculum*, edited by P. W. Jackson. New York: Macmillan.

Spady, W. G. (October 1988). "Organizing for Results: The Basis of Authentic Restructuring." *Educational Leadership* 46, 2: 4–8.

Spady, W. G., and K. J. Marshall. (October 1991). "Beyond Traditional Outcome-Based Education." *Educational Leadership* 48, 2: 67–72.

Stasz, C., K. Ramsey, R. Eden, J. DaVanzo, H. Farris, and M. Lewis. (1993). *Classrooms That Work: Teaching Generic Skills in Academic and Vocational Settings.* Santa Monica, Calif.: Rand.

Tyler, R. W. (1949). *Basic Principles of Curriculum and Instruction.* Chicago: University of Chicago Press.

Vars, G. F. (October 1991). "Integrated Curriculum in Historical Perspective."

Educational Leadership 49, 2: 14–15.

Walberg, H. J. (March 1988). "Synthesis of Research on Time and Learning." *Educational Leadership* 45, 6: 76–86.

Walker, D. F., and J. Schaffarzick. (Sept.-Oct. 1974). "Comparing Curricula." *Review of Educational Research* 44, 1: 83–112.

Wang, M. C., G. D. Haertel, and H. J. Walberg. (1990). "What Influences Learning? A Content Analysis of Review Literature." *Journal of Educational Research* 84, 1: 30–43.

Wang, M. C., G. D. Haertel, and H. M. Walberg. (1993). "What Helps Students Learn?" *Educational Leadership* 51, 4: 74–79.

Wilkerson, R. M., and K. P. White. (March 1988). "Effects of the 4MAT System of Instruction on Students' Achievement, Retention, and Attitudes." *Elementary School Journal* 88, 4: 357–368.

Specific Audit Issues for the Quality Curriculum Criteria

The information included here has been derived from a review of the research and the current literature. The primary source for the criterion under review is noted at the end of each section.

Issues for Quality Curriculum-Related Learning

1. Curriculum-referenced test results indicate significant gain in a year's time in the major subjects.
2. Students report positive feelings about their educational experiences and the subjects they are studying.
3. Employers and colleges report general satisfaction with graduates' skill and knowledge.
4. Parents report general satisfaction with their children's educational experiences.

Primary Source: Wang, M. C., G. D. Haertel, and H. J. Walberg. (1993). "What Helps Students Learn?" *Educational Leadership* 51, 4: 74-79.

Issues for Quality Curriculum-Related Teaching

The quality of curriculum-related teaching is first assessed by observing student learning; the observer then analyzes the extent to which the teaching is facilitating desirable learning practices.

1. Did the learners seem motivated to learn? Did the teacher seem sensitive to the importance of intrinsic motivation by helping students find meaning and purpose in what was to be learned?

2. Did the learners understand and internalize the learning goal? Was the learning objective curriculum-related, meaningful to the student, and clear to all? Did the teacher select an appropriate goal and help students internalize it?

3. Did the learners activate their prior knowledge? Did the teacher assist in this process and facilitate it?

4. Did the learners acquire new knowledge? Did the teacher provide means for acquiring that knowledge that were both efficient and effective?

5. Did the learners relate the new knowledge to prior knowledge and modify knowledge constructs accordingly? Did the teacher facilitate this process?

6. Did the learners construct personal meaning by organizing, elaborating, and representing knowledge in their own way? Did the teacher facilitate this process?

7. Did the learners identify a complex problem to be solved and solve that problem by making knowledge generative? Did the teacher facilitate this process?

8. Did the learners seem to have an appropriate amount of scaffolding and structuring from the teacher in solving the problem?

9. Did the learners understand and use the strategies needed to solve the problem? Did the teacher provide the necessary help in this process?

10. Did the learners learn in a supportive social context? Did the teacher facilitate reflective dialogue, cooperative inquiry, and the social construction of knowledge?

11. Did the learners use metacognitive monitoring to assess their learning processes? Did the teacher facilitate this process?

12. Did the learners assess their learning and demonstrate their understanding? Did the teacher make periodic assessments of learning and use assessment data to adjust instruction and remediate when necessary?

Primary Source: Brooks, J. G., and M. G. Brooks. (1983). *In Search of Understanding: The Case for Constructivist Classrooms.* Alexandria, Va.: Association for Supervision and Curriculum Development.

Issues for Quality Curriculum Guides

Format
1. Is the guide easy to use? Is it "teacher friendly"?

Emphases
2. Does the guide make explicit the values that inform it—the view of knowledge that it represents?
3. Does the content of the guide reflect sound research in that field and the recommendations of experts?
4. Does the guide emphasize depth of profound knowledge (instead of coverage), the acquisition of useful skills, and the application of that knowledge and those skills in solving meaningful problems?
5. Do the overall structure and content of the guide reflect and contribute to the district's vision of a curriculum of excellence?
6. Does the guide focus on meaningful outcomes that enable all students to succeed in higher education and develop the requisite career skills?
7. Does the guide develop in students an appreciation of diversity, a valuing of our common heritage, and a concern for equity?

Placement and Sequence
8. Are the grade-level objectives developmentally appropriate?
9. Does the guide provide for a meaningful sequence and coordination of learning, without excessive repetition?

Organization and Structure
10. Does the guide clearly indicate the goals for that subject and how those subject goals relate to the district's educational goals?
11. Are the grade-level objectives derived from subject goals, and are they clearly stated?
12. Does the guide include other materials that teachers have requested, such as learning resources?
13. Does the guide provide for and facilitate the appropriate integration of knowledge within that subject and from related subjects?

Articulation and Coordination

14. Are there mechanisms in place and materials available to ensure that what is taught in a particular subject at a particular grade level builds upon what was taught at a prior grade level and leads to what will be taught at the next grade level, without excessive repetition?

15. Are there mechanisms in place and materials available to ensure that at a given grade level subjects that depend upon each other are congruent in the skills and knowledge taught?

Primary Source: Glatthorn, A. A. (1993). *Criteria for Evaluating Curriculum Guides.* Greenville, N.C.: School of Education, East Carolina University.

Issues for Quality Curriculum Implementation

1. Does the district have a systematic process for implementing new curriculums?

2. Does the district provide teachers with the staff development needed to implement the new curriculum?

3. Do principals provide a leadership role in the implementation stage, supporting the new curriculum, encouraging its use, monitoring implementation, and ensuring that teachers have the help needed?

4. Has the curriculum guide been aligned with tests and texts, and do teachers make effective use of such alignment materials?

5. Has the district provided in a timely manner the materials needed to implement the new curriculum?

Primary Source: Snyder, J., F. Boline, and K. Zumwalt. (1992). "Curriculum Implementation." In *Handbook of Research on Curriculum,* edited by P. W. Jackson. New York: Macmillan.

Issues for Quality Scheduling

Time

1. In elementary schools, does the district or the school provide guidelines for the teacher's allocation of time to the several subjects, and do those allocations reflect the district's curricular priorities? In secondary schools, does the schedule show time allocations that reflect the district's priorities?

2. Does the district or the school provide teachers with guidelines for the allocation of time to areas of the curriculum within a given subject?

3. Do principals defend instructional time by eliminating unnecessary intrusions?

Grouping

4. Do the grouping practices facilitate student learning and the development of self-esteem, avoiding inflexible grouping and tracking practices that stigmatize and limit opportunities?

Staffing

5. Are teachers provided with a teachable schedule that limits the number of their preparations, provides them with adequate and suitable space, and facilitates effective teaching?

6. Does the schedule provide adequate time for teachers to plan together?

Primary Source: Glatthorn, A. A. (1986). "How Does the School Schedule Affect Curriculum?" In *Rethinking Reform: The Principal's Dilemma,* edited by H. J. Walberg and J. W. Keefe. Reston, Va.: National Association of Secondary School Principals.

Issues for Quality Teacher Planning

1. Do teachers develop effective yearly plans that indicate unit titles and goals, the sequence of units, and time allocations?

2. Do teachers develop unit plans that appropriately integrate content within and across subjects and emphasize the solving of meaningful and contextualized problems?

3. Do teachers systematically deliver daily lessons that are well organized and effectively structured?

Primary Source: Glatthorn, A. A. (1993). "Teacher Planning: A Foundation for Effective Instruction." *NASSP Bulletin* 77, 551: 1-7.

Issues for Quality Learning Materials

1. Has the district provided quality learning materials that are closely aligned with the curriculum guides?
2. Do the materials provide students with alternative learning resources that supplement print materials?
3. Are the learning materials free of ethnic and gender bias?
4. Can students read the materials while still being challenged to grow in their reading skills?
5. Do the materials reflect best current practice in that subject?

Primary Source: Muther, C. (program consultant). *The Pitfalls of Textbook Adoption and How to Avoid Them* (videotape and user's manual). (1985). Alexandria, Va.: Association for Supervision and Curriculum Development.

Issues for Quality Professional Development

1. Has the district provided principals with leadership training in the area of curriculum?
2. Have teachers had access to quality staff development programs at both the district and school levels that enable them to implement the curriculum and facilitate learning effectively?
3. Are teachers provided with supervision that responds to their individual needs and offers options for growth?
4. Are staff development and supervision programs linked directly to school improvement efforts?

Primary Source: Fullan, M. G. (1990). "Staff Development, Innovation, and Institutional Achievement." In *Challenges and Achievements of American Education,* edited by B. Joyce. Alexandria, Va.: Association for Supervision and Curriculum Development.

Issues for Quality Curriculum Leadership

1. Do principals understand their leadership role and carry out that role effectively?
2. Is there effective curriculum leadership at the district level?
3. Do teachers have ready access to subject-matter expertise when needed?

Primary Source: Cotton, K. (1990). *Effective Schooling Practices: A Research Synthesis, 1990 Update.* Portland, Ore.: Northwest Regional Educational Laboratory.

Issues for Quality Program Evaluation

1. Has the district developed curriculum-referenced tests that are closely aligned with the curriculum?
2. Do district tests emphasize performance and demonstration of learning?
3. Do teachers make use of curriculum-referenced test results to improve their teaching?
4. Does the district make use of curriculum-referenced test results to improve the curriculum?
5. Are curriculums evaluated systematically and periodically for their effectiveness?
6. Does the district rigorously evaluate curriculum guides before they are disseminated for teacher use, and does such an evaluation include pilot testing?

Primary Source: Herman, J. L., L. L. Morris, and C. T. Fitz-Gibbon. (1987). *Evaluator's Handbook.* Newbury Park, Calif.: Sage.

About the Author

Allan A. Glatthorn is professor of education at East Carolina University. He has served as a consultant in curriculum to more than one hundred school systems and is the author of several books and articles on curriculum.

Index